# Cutting the Ties
## that Bind

## Epigraph

*"Freedom is independence from externals. One who is in need of the help of another person, thing or condition is a slave thereof. Perfect freedom is not given to any man on earth, because the very meaning of mortal life is relationship with and dependence on another. The lesser number of wants, the greater is the freedom. Hence perfect freedom is absolute desirelessness.*

*SRI SATHYA SAI BABA*

# Cutting the Ties
## that Bind

*Growing up and Moving on*

PHYLLIS KRYSTAL

Concern in Love
SAI TOWERS
PUBLISHING

First Indian Edition 1997

First Reprint 2003
Second Reprint 2006
Third Reprint 2008
Fourth Reprint 2013

ISBN - 81-86822-33-X

Published and distributed by:
**Sai Towers Publishing**
Sai Towers
3/604, Main Road, Prasanthi Nilayam, 515 134 INDIA
Phone: +91 (8555) 287 270/287 327/287 329
E-mail : publishing@saitowers.com
Web : www.saitowers.com

BRITISH LIBRARY CATALOGUING IN PUBLICATION DATA
A CATALOGUE RECORD OF THIS BOOK IS AVAILABLE FROM THE BRITISH LIBRARY

Printed in India at **Vishruthi Prints,** Bangalore

# CONTENTS

Preface                                                                    xiii
Introduction                                                                xiv

Chapter
1.   The Method of Working                                                   1
2.   The Core of the Work                                                    5
3.   Preparation for the First Inner Session                                12
4.   Puberty Rite—Cutting the Ties to One Parent                            22
5.   Dealing with Negative Parental Archetypes                              35
6.   Positive and Negative Attributes of Parents                            40
7.   Connecting to Inner Cosmic Parents                                     48
8.   The Inner Child                                                        56
9.   Animus and Anima: Male and Female Aspects
     within Women and Men                                                   69
10.  Cutting Ties to Other Relationships                                    76
11.  Releasing from Negative Forces                                         86
12.  The Inner Enemy                                                        92
13.  The Inner House                                                        98
14.  The Mandala                                                           102
15.  Dreams and What They Mean                                             111
16.  Corridor of Doors                                                     123
17.  Death and Death Rites                                                 127
18.  Symbols and How to Use Them                                           139

Conclusion                                                                175
Index                                                                     177
About the Author                                                          181

*I dedicate this book to Sri Sathya Sai Baba who exemplifies in human form the High Consciousness inherent within everyone and everything.*

# PREFACE

It will be easier for the reader to understand this book if he or she will bear in mind that it deals primarily with symbols. A symbol is a device by which a message can be carried effectively to the subconscious part of the mind. Symbols are effective because the language of the subconscious mind is composed of symbols and pictures.

The subconscious mind is primitive or childlike and the symbols used to communicate with it should be chosen accordingly. Just as children learn more quickly and easily in a relaxed atmosphere through play and games, so the childlike part of the mind thrives when appropriate methods are used to impress upon it whatever the conscious mind wishes it to understand and carry out.

Rituals with their underlying messages also impress the subconscious mind, especially if they are charged with emotion and performed in a serious manner. The techniques, rituals and symbols presented in this book are all capable of impressing positive messages on the subconscious mind in order to offset some of the negative conditioning that may have been received earlier in life.

The reader will therefore benefit to a greater degree if criticism or evaluation are held in abeyance: the various techniques should not be dismissed as being too childish to be effective. By consciously withholding judgement, the reader's subconscious mind will be allowed an opportunity to participate and benefit from the positive conditioning presented by the symbols. Unless the subconscious mind is impressed, no changes can be made in a person's life, no matter how much he may consciously desire to change and evolve.

# ACKNOWLEDGEMENTS

I acknowledge the help of all the people who have worked with me, whose problems and questions have elicited answers which have resulted in the development of the techniques outlined in this book.

# INTRODUCTION

This book presents a method by which liberation from all the various sources of false security can be achieved. This method enables a person to become an independent and whole human being, relying only on the inner source of security and wisdom which is available to everyone who seeks its aid. This discipline is the culmination of an experiment of more than twenty years, started by another woman and myself. We first met while we were both engaged in investigating various methods which we hoped would help us to find more meaning to life.

We discovered that we were both dissatisfied and disillusioned with the lack of convincing answers to some of our serious questions about life. "Why are we here? Who are we? Where are we going?" we asked, feeling there must surely be some practical way to seek further for answers to such questions. We had both learned a reverie or waking dream technique and decided to use it to ask to be shown anything which would be helpful for us to experience or be taught. We met regularly, alternating roles; one time one of us directed and the other received the impressions, the next time the process was reversed.

One of the very first things we were shown was the use of a triangle as a basis from which to work, to link us to the High Self in order to seek guidance from this wisdom within each of us. This source of wisdom is always available but will not interfere in our lives or go against our free will unless we ask for its help.

To set the stage for this, we both visualized a line of light connecting the two of us at ground level, with one of us at point A and the other opposite at B. We then imagined a line of light going up our spines, out through the top of each of our heads, and on up to meet at C, the apex of our triangle. This point C represented for us the meeting place with our High Self, where we are one. In time we began to call this point C the 'High C' (for High Consciousness) and, from then on, we always gave over each session to its direction, asking to be given whatever we needed and could handle at that particular time.

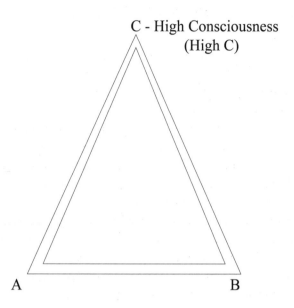

C - High Consciousness
(High C)

A                                    B

Experience from working with many different types of people has proved that this term, 'High C', is acceptable to everyone, whatever their background. Most people who are seeking for meaning of life have some idea, however vague, that there is a power within everyone which transcends the limited conscious personality. That they are seeking help in the first place indicates that they have obviously come to the realization that their conscious minds and brains are not capable of helping them handle all their problems. Usually they gratefully agree to seek further help from the indwelling wisdom when they are shown ways to contact it.

Working with the High C in this way is the basic difference between this and most other methods, in which the conscious mind of the doctor or therapist is usually the authority and the counselling takes place across the base of a triangle, or from one conscious mind to the other.

From our work over the years we have accumulated a large body of material on many different subjects, including answers to questions and techniques to use to help ourselves and others with personal problems. At first we rarely mentioned what we were doing as it would have been considered strange in the *1950s* and 1960s. But now that the psychic and spiritual explosion has taken place, it has become quite fashionable. Since that early beginning, other interested seekers would join us from time to time, some working for a while to solve their problems and then moving on, having learned effective ways to continue to help themselves. A few people delved deeper into the work, helping to uncover more and more teaching and techniques as they sought help for their own lives.

Now many people, particularly the younger ones, are becoming seriously interested in self-discovery. Some of them are finding their way to this work. It is hoped that they will be the ones who will use the methods we have been taught, in order to uncover more answers and practical ways to help them in their quest for wholeness. They can then pass on their findings to others and thus help to spread the teaching still further. The method is not crystallized or static, but is continually expanding as more people use it.

This book presents the method, the various techniques and rituals for achieving release from old attachments and patterns, as well as some of the teachings we have received so that these may be shared with more people than can be reached personally. This is. therefore, a handbook for lay people as well as professional therapists, because it is absolutely safe to use this method if the directions are followed carefully, and the help of the High C is sought. Many of the people who have benefited from the work have urged me time and again to write a book about it. At first I was dismayed at the thought as I am not a professional writer and had grave doubts about my ability to write a book, so I asked for advice in one of the sessions. I was assured that the book had already taken shape during the years of work and needed only to be put into tangible form in a simple and straightforward style.

So I hope that everyone who reads this book and decides to make use of it will discover that it will lead to as much of an adventure and will prove to be as great a blessing as it has been for all those who have helped it to develop this far.

*Phyllis Krystal*

Chapter 1

# THE METHOD OF WORKING

This book describes a method which has been developed to enable two people working together to tap into knowledge and teaching beyond the conscious mind of either of them. The state of mind during the work has been likened to a waking dream or active imagination, but neither of these terms gives an accurate description. Those who have experienced it invariably describe the state they are in as heightened awareness and comment on the fact that the emotions experienced are usually far more intense than those encountered in ordinary consciousness, the mental pictures far more vivid.

I must make two points absolutely clear from the start: first, the participants are fully awake and conscious of everything they are experiencing, are never in a trance, and remember in detail everything that transpired during each session. Secondly, it is not necessary to be specially gifted or psychic, that is, clairvoyant, clairaudient, or mediumistic, to do this work. The requirements for each partner are a sincere desire to seek the truth, honesty, dedication, obedience to the inner guidance, and willingness to set aside the ego, personal will and desires, and pet beliefs or biases, so that the teaching from the High C can flow through as untainted by the human vehicles as possible.

While two of us were working one day, I was given an interesting picture to illustrate the necessity of being absolutely open, with the ego as much out of the way as possible. We were, as usual, asking to be shown whatever was appropriate and timely for either of us for that day. The only picture I was receiving was of an urn which stayed firmly in front of my inner gaze and did not fade or disappear. As I concentrated on it, I became aware that it was badly cracked and chipped, and the thought crossed my mind that it would leak if water were poured into it. I asked why I was being shown this battered old urn. The answer came like a flash and really shocked me. Suddenly, I knew that it represented me, and that we are all chipped and cracked. I then realized with relief that this need not affect our ability to do this work. Since we are making contact with the light within each of us to dispel the darkness of ignorance, this light can be seen even better through the cracks, and can more easily radiate out to others. From then on, I stopped worrying that I might not be adequate to work in this way or be a clear channel.

The requirements for each team of two are, first, a rapport between them, which forms the base of the triangle they will be using to contact the High C. It is also important that they be disciplined enough to work regularly and, above all, have a minimum of competitiveness or one-upmanship, since it is the inner knowledge that is being sought, not that of either partner. Differences in the personalities of two workers can be helpful, as they allow for greater polarity and lessen the danger of either one going off at a tangent. Also, such differences sometimes produce an interesting situation when each partner receives a picture or impression which, at first glance, appears to contradict the other but which turns out to contain the same message expressed differently; the messages are therefore mutually corroborative. Sometimes the picture seen by each partner separately, when put together, forms a whole message, each being but a part.

As we proceeded, it gradually became apparent that the work could be used in many different ways. From the very beginning, we were told that we must be willing to share what we were being taught with anyone who was open to it and would use it. So, in addition to the regular meetings for our own guidance and teaching, which were rather like attending a school of higher learning, we worked with various people who came to us seeking help and advice for their problems.

Sometimes one or the other of us would work directly with those seeking help, either by both tuning into the High C, or often by sharing with them from the teachings we had been given earlier. Sometimes we helped people to decipher dreams or proceeded with whatever seemed applicable for the particular person and problem. At other times, two of us would work together, asking to be shown how best to help those seeking guidance. This method was used primarily for those living at a distance or who were not available to work with one of us directly. In such cases, the results of our work were passed on to them either by telephone or letter and the recommended mental exercises or meditations explained to them. We have been repeatedly warned against taking over and doing all the work for others as this would only strengthen our mental and spiritual muscles instead of theirs.

The many and varied problems brought to our attention were often the means by which we were given new teaching on a very large number of diverse subjects. As we began to use whatever teaching we were given, we learned to trust the source, especially when we saw the many proofs of it working in peoples' lives.

Gradually, by word of mouth, more people heard about our activities. Among them were several psychologists who would call on us to help them with some of their more difficult or particularly puzzling cases. My elder daughter, a licensed psychologist, had personally benefited from the work and uses the various techniques and exercises with her clients with excellent results. In addition, she and I meet regularly to ask the High C for further insights and instructions to aid her in diagnosing her clients' problems and to facilitate her working with them more effectively. She offers this service only to those clients whom she feels are open to the work, who give their permission, and who are willing to follow the guidance received in this way. Most of them eagerly grasp at the extra help and insight and as a result my daughter is better able to help them help themselves, which is the key to their healing and growth. They soon see how the work accelerates the healing process and we usually have a long list of requests each time we meet.

It is from this work that a pattern has emerged which can be used by psychotherapists and counsellors, and which will be discussed in detail in this book. We are hoping that more therapists will, in time, make use of the greater wisdom which is available when the High C is evoked by both therapist and client.

One situation which is invariably encountered in counselling is that of projection or transference. This is lessened when both client and therapist rely on the High C as the authority instead of on the therapist, and when both practise a visualization exercise which we have been given to reduce this particular problem. We call this exercise the 'Figure Eight' and its uses will be described in detail in the text.

Chapter 2

# THE CORE OF THE WORK

It was during one of the sessions with my daughter, when we were about to ask for insight into several of her clients, that, quite unexpectedly, the core or main theme of this book was presented.

As soon as we were quiet, and after she had read aloud the list of names of those requesting insights and we had mentally erected the triangle between us, I instantly saw, as if on an inner screen, what looked like a zoo or circus, with many cages, each housing a different animal. As I watched this inner picture, I was fascinated by the many different ways in which the animals reacted to their confinement. Some of the big cats paced nervously up and down, graceful but frustrated; some animals threw themselves against the bars of their cages in obvious rage and rebellion, frantic and frightened, desperately trying to escape. Other animals would slink into the back of the cage and curl up into a ball like an embryo, withdrawing from all participation in living. Some went on a hunger strike, refusing to eat; while others, like the bears, were performing, doing tricks and putting on a show for visitors to attract attention and to distract themselves from their boredom. Others were ingratiating, rolling over and begging for food from their keepers. As I watched such varied reactions, I wondered why I was being shown this picture and became immediately aware that people, like the animals I was seeing, are all imprisoned in cages, but of their own making. I also knew, with an inner certainty, that they can attain freedom from their cages if they so desire.

Would anyone actually not want to be free, I wondered? In answer, my mind was drawn to several people I knew who would certainly fit that category. As I looked further, I realized that many people resist any kind of change, preferring the security of an habitual situation or condition, however difficult or unhappy, to the insecurity of something unknown and different from that which they were used to handling. There are also those who protest that they want to be free, but when they are offered the opportunity to escape from their prisons they find that they do not really want freedom strongly enough to be willing to relinquish their attachments to people, possessions, desires, security, or any thing which they cannot live without. People will go to great lengths to protect their cherished dreams and desires, and will fight any attempt to show them that these are often at the root of their unhappiness.

I was next aware that, like Ariadne's thread, one must allow the process to lead back to the cause, past the smoke screen of protest by the conscious mind, to seek the key which can unlock each person's prison; for only by discovering the hidden cause of the symptoms is the healing likely to be lasting. The ego with its 'I want' and 'I don't want' is a deep-seated core which is fiercely protected, like a citadel, with anger, fear and desperation before capitulation to the High Self takes place.

This surrender to the inner wisdom is the key to health and wholeness and is the true meaning of "Thy will, not mine, be done" "Thy will" refers to the will of our own High Self, which alone knows why each person is in this life, whereas "my will" is the compulsive personal will of the ego with its attachments to myriads of desires.

I realized that we are given free will, but look where it usually lands us: in cages! Until we realize that we are free only when we learn to trust the High C, we cannot really know what freedom means. The precept "Let trust in that higher wisdom storm the embattled citadel of the small self", flashed into my mind I saw that all psychological problems and unhappiness are merely signs to point the way to the inner conflict and, if understood correctly, can lead back to its root cause. As I looked around, I realized that everyone alive suffers from some aspect of this 'sickness of separation from the High C'. Some people are more severely affected than others, some manage more successfully to camouflage it, or hide from it by resorting to various ploys, such as constant activity, drugs, alcohol, sex, television, books, or eating. How like those animals in their cages we all are! I was awed by the picture.

Then I recalled the Eastern philosophies and their insistence on desirelessness and detachment, and I saw that in our work we have been shown how to cut the ties which bind us to things, people, places, ways of life, to anything which prevents us from being free. I further realized that the techniques which have been revealed to us as we worked all these years are the means by which we can escape from our cages, and help others to do likewise.

Then I was given a brief experience of this eventual freedom and I recognized it as being identical to a level of consciousness I have attained from time to time for short periods during the work sessions, and which I have always referred to as the 'tapestry level'.

At times, when I was focusing on the images or thoughts I was receiving, I would suddenly be aware of a tremendous change in my attitude. I would feel as if I were floating freely in space in a pink glow, like a bird riding the wind, as I looked down at a most beautiful tapestry. I always enjoyed these brief times at that level of consciousness and felt I was being given a god's eye view of the world which never ceased to amaze me. I would sometimes try to go there consciously, but was never able to do so as reaching this state seems to be beyond conscious control. At first, I was also a little horrified at my change of attitude. As I looked down at man's inhumanity to man, all the wars, murders, rapes, and sorrows, I would really feel that, despite such horrors, as Browning put it, "God's in His heaven, All's right with the world!". A few minutes earlier I would have been bowed down with depression by the world scene; but at this other level I was, for a moment, free of the world and could observe it all in perspective, knowing that everything is inevitable for the very necessary learning it alone makes possible.

Seen from above, the tapestry was always very beautiful, with brilliant colours, both dark and light, all woven harmoniously together to create an intricate pattern; everything in its proper place. However, this same tapestry looked at from below, from our limited conscious view, was very different: the pattern looked blurred and indistinct as the many knots and loose ends of thread obscured the beautiful design I had seen from above, and all the colours seemed to run together. It became clear that from the High C view the real pattern is visible.

Our lives intertwine with one another's for our mutual learning, and we attract to ourselves those people and experiences we need to teach us whatever it is we need to learn. Because we cannot see beyond our limited view, the pattern seems to us to be ugly and untidy and, therefore, wrong. But seen from above, where the design is clear, all is as it is, and must be, and as we have all woven it. Even the negative aspects are inevitable parts of the whole.

Then I realized that 'even the knots are right', a phrase we have used many, many times to illustrate the point that seemingly negative experiences are often exactly what we need to push us out of our ruts and force us to grow. There is a strong tendency in most people to relax and take life easy if things go too smoothly for them. This leads to stagnation and prevents growth. It is only because we cannot see the beautiful woven pattern we are all hoping to make, but see only the negative-looking underside, that we judge it wrongly.

When I was sharing this picture one day with a young woman who had come to see me while still in deep sorrow over the loss of a loved one, she asked, from her anguish, "But wouldn't the view you describe make us all uncaring and indifferent?".

I knew exactly what she meant, because that had been my own fear at first; but experience has proven otherwise. On the contrary, it actually brings out more compassion and a greater understanding, and it reduces criticism of others, which are the only attitudes with which to offer help.

One young man who found himself at the tapestry level while we were working one day had a different reaction. He did not want to leave it and return to "the ordinary drab consciousness of daily life", as he expressed it, any more than those who take drugs to escape the tedium, dullness, fear and ugliness of their lives want to give the drugs up.

We have been cautioned over and over again that only by living in a human body in this mundane world can we work on ourselves to attain the goal of freedom glimpsed at the tapestry level. We must work to earn the right to stay there permanently. If we withdraw from life in any way, we only delay our progress.

The key which opens the door of the cages in which we are trapped is found only in the cage which itself is imprisoned in the world in which we live. The way to find the key is to dig deep within ourselves to discover where we are holding on to the bars and, therefore, to what things, people or beliefs we are attached.

As soon as I understood the significance of the caged animal scene, I realized that the instruction and tools which we had already been given over the years were perfectly designed to help all those who seek freedom from false security to release from whatever was keeping them imprisoned in a cage.

The caged animal scene is indeed the core of the work and provides the central theme around which it can be described. In order to be completely free, we need to be detached from anyone or anything which binds or dominates us, or in which we seek to find security in preference to the High C within each of us.

I then recalled that Jesus told the rich man to leave his parents, wife and home and follow him. I now understood that this does not necessarily mean to leave them literally or physically by deserting them and neglecting responsibilities which have been assumed. Rather, it appeared that it can also refer to detachment from dependence on family, which often prevents absolute reliance on the High C and the freedom to follow its will and direction instead of the will of the ego or that of another person.

A major part of our work involves cutting the cords or tie connecting us to anything or anyone in whom we place our trust and which therefore become gods for us. Because these lesser god are impermanent and can be taken from us, they are unreliable as a source of security. It is not important whether these bond were forged by love, need, pity, fear, hate or any other emotion What is important is that they have the power to keep us dependent on the things to which they attach us instead of on the High C

During the years of work a pattern or sequence of steps emerged which formed a method that can be used by pairs of people working together to free themselves for mutual growth. This method provides a system which can be used by professional therapist with their clients, the High C adding an important dimension that can greatly accelerate the process of healing.

When a human being is willing to reach up in consciousness to make contact with the indwelling source of wisdom and healing, his work, whatever its nature, is necessarily refined and strengthened as it is raised beyond the domination of the ego. It is just as necessary for the therapist as it is for the client to ask the High C for guidance because help can be found more easily when they are both sincerely willing to seek the aid of the High C common to both of them.

We have been shown many different ties or bonds which will be discussed in the following chapters, together with instructions for detaching from them, which often include the revival of old puberty rites which have been allowed to fall into disuse in our present culture.

The first ties are those forged during childhood to parents or guardians, close relatives, siblings, teachers, friends and any others who help to influence, or programme the child. Later ties are formed to friends, lovers, marriage partners, other family members, children, and anyone on whom we rely for security, whether living or dead. There are also more subtle attachments, to having one's own way or to one's own opinions, as well as to strong emotions such as anger, jealousy, fear and pride. Attachments can also be formed with appetites for such things as food, alcohol, drugs, money, jewels, clothes, houses, cars, power, social status, education, success to name but a few. And lastly, attachment to life itself makes so many people so terrified of death.

We have often observed that when a person has really achieved detachment while still living in this world, death is a very simple and unfrightening event. As the dying person releases from the physical body, he is free to move on into another dimension of consciousness without the temptation to remain too close to the attachments to the earth scene, as well as to the emotional pull exerted by those people who are about to be deprived of his physical presence.

Thus it can be seen that the work is a continuing process, whereby a person can go as far as he wishes in the relinquishment of ties. If followed all the way, it can lead to release from all desires and, finally, from the wheel of rebirth. However, few people accomplish this in one lifetime, and not everyone would want to; but that need not deter anyone from using this method to free themselves sufficiently to handle their problems, improve their situation and relationships, and lead a more fulfilling life.

Chapter 3

# PREPARATION
# FOR THE
# FIRST INNER SESSION

## Ties to Parents

When meeting with a new person, we first try to discover why he has come for this type of help. People hear about this work only from others who have benefited from it, so they are, to a certain extent, aware of what is involved. As soon as we begin to see the nature of the problem, we explain that the person must look at his own attitudes first, as he can be helped to gain control over them, which is often sufficient to improve the situation.

We then explain that most problems stem from often unconscious reactions to early training, and we invariably start a person to work on these by helping him to release from his parents using what we loosely call 'puberty rites' or 'cutting the connecting cords'. Not only does this free him from unhealthy dependence, but also from the often negative programming by parents, which had still been active on a deep unconscious level, preventing him from knowing himself. This first session gives him an opportunity to experience the different state of consciousness which we refer to as waking dream or reverie, and at the same time gives the person who is conducting the session a good idea of how the person is likely to participate in this kind of work.

Naturally, the very first bonds are formed to the parents because they were the channels through whom we achieved birth. A strong early link is very important during the first few years of life when the child needs this security as a firm base from which to develop.

A custom is now being revived called bonding, by which these ties are reinforced shortly after birth. It has been found that a baby is fully conscious, its eyes open and able to focus, for about twenty minutes immediately following birth. With the various natural childbirth methods now being used, in which both parents are present and the mother is fully awake, the baby is locked into both parents by direct eye contact as soon as possible.

However, at puberty, when the young person is about to enter the world as an adult, the early ties to the parents used to be severed so that the youth is free to develop as an independent individual. Unfortunately, in our society, many of the old customs and rituals have fallen into disuse. This is especially true of the puberty and death rites. When still used, they are often so diluted and superficial that they are useless for all practical purposes, and continue to be observed only as empty shells, lacking the original symbolic meaning and therefore reduced to the status of social functions.

We describe to each new person how we conduct this ritual and explain that it can be performed at any time after puberty regardless of age, since it is rarely accomplished in depth at the normal time. We refer to the old customs still in use in some primitive societies today, which are closer to their original form, and we stress how important it is for a young person about to attain maturity to be taken from the parents and the world of childhood and introduced into the life of the village as a young adult.

When these ties have remained uncut beyond the age of puberty, an unhealthy situation often develops where the child, whatever his age, is either too dependent on one or both parents and, therefore, incapable of expressing his own true personality, or has rebelled violently and broken away from the parents with hard feelings on both sides. The latter situation can result in extra negative ties which can bind even more tightly than the original more positive ones.

When presented with this information, people react very differently, depending on their experience and background. Some will protest that they have already broken away and achieved their independence, often describing the drastic means they used to accomplish this. However, we have found that they are rarely free and that estrangement, distance and even death of the parents do not necessarily free them. In fact, such a person is often even more strongly attached, despite their belief to the contrary. Others, when they are told about the need to cut the cords, react very differently and express great relief at hearing that it is never too late to be free, whatever age they are.

I recall one woman in her forties who has a particularly domineering matriarch of a mother, blurting out, "If you can help me break away from my mother, most of my problems will be solved." Another person, a young man, reacted with, "I moved three thousand miles to get away from my father, without success; I can still feel him criticizing me across the miles."

Still others recoil at the very idea of separation, believing that close family ties are sacred, despite the often smothering and stultifying effect the ties may have on the different individuals who make up the family group. Then there are a few who hate the very thought of being pushed out of the nest, preferring the security it provides to the independence of being out in the world on their own.

Sometimes a person will have been brought up by relatives, family friends, or by foster parents or institutions. In such cases, we find that there is often a deep-seated unconscious resentment towards the real parents and that a feeling of rejection colours their lives. Such people have to be taken through the separation from their real parents, but also from the proxy parents who reared them.

It is impossible for any parents to be perfect for all their children and even the best of them still need to be released if their offspring are to become independent adults. So, even if there is a minimum of friction, it is wise to make the severance of ties as it invariably improves the relationship by allowing it to be more free and flowing.

As in the old rituals, there are preparations which need to be undertaken before the actual cutting of the cords can be undertaken. A preliminary exercise has been given to us for this purpose. It must be practised regularly every day for a period of not less than two weeks for each parent or guardian. We call this exercise the Figure Eight, as it looks like the number 8. It is used to draw each person in a close relationship into his own space or territory and it has become one of our most useful symbols.

Two people who have a close relationship with one another invariably project part of themselves onto the other so that neither is a clear-cut and separate individual. If they were to cut the cords between them before a withdrawal of each into his own space had been achieved, the result would be confused, as each person would still be carrying the projections from the other like an overlay covering the real self. To remedy this situation we were given the Figure Eight exercise, which I will describe as if I were explaining it to someone for the first time.

### Instructions for Visualizing the Figure Eight

"Before cutting the ties between you and your parents, the following exercise must be practised daily for at least two weeks for each parent.

Close your eyes and settle comfortably in your chair or on the floor and imagine that you are drawing a circle around you *on the ground* at arm's length, so that the radius of the circle is the length of your arm with fingers extended. Visualize this circle as a tube of gold light, like sunlight. Do not hurry or strain to see it, but rather allow it to appear in your mind's eye.

When you are satisfied that you are in the centre of a circle of gold light, visualize a similar circle just barely touching your own, but not overlapping yours. Now see which one of your parents appears in the circle in front of your own when you call for one or the other of them.

Be sure that each of you stays in the very middle of your own circle and, if it appears to you that either of you moves from the centre or tries to enter the other's space, imagine that both of you are like puppets or dolls which can be picked up and put back where they belong. You may have to do this several times before you both stay. centred, especially in a situation where one is more dominant than the other.

When you can see the two circles clearly, and both of you are in the centre of your own space, visualize a pale blue neon light flowing inside the golden tube, starting at the point where the two circles join and moving in a clockwise direction, first around your parent's circle directly in front of you and back to where the circles meet. Now watch the blue light continue on around the left side of your own circle, around behind you to your right, and then back again to where they meet, making a figure eight. Continue to watch this flow of blue light in your mind's eye for as long as you can hold the picture without strain. This varies with each person but is rarely more than two minutes. The blue neon light will magnetically draw all of you into your circle and all of your parent into his or her's, so that each of you will occupy fully your own separate territory.

This exercise must be repeated regularly every day until it flows easily, ensuring that the message that you wish to become an independent individual penetrates to the subconscious mind of both your parent and yourself. The subconscious mind understands

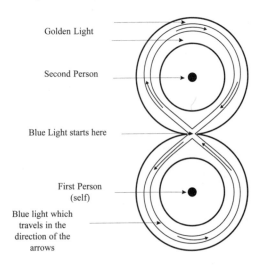

Golden Light

Second Person

Blue Light starts here

First Person
(self)

Blue light which
travels in the
direction of the
arrows

THE FIGURE EIGHT

pictures and symbols more easily than words, but they have to be regularly repeated for the intended message to be received and acted upon. The times best suited for beaming messages in this way are just as you are awakening from sleep and again as you are about to enter the sleep state, when you are closest to your subconscious mind.

After you have the picture clearly established, just a short practice period of about two minutes night and morning is sufficient. During the rest of the day, it is helpful to visualize giving your Figure Eight a little push to keep it moving, in the same way that a child bowling a wooden hoop will give a gentle tap with the stick to keep it rolling.

Please do not hesitate to check back with me if you have any problems with this exercise so that you can be sure you are doing it correctly from the start.

It is interesting to hear the various reports as people work with this symbol. Many times a particular dominant parent will appear to try to move into the 'child's' circle, while sometimes the 'child' will be surprised to see that he is the one who is trying to move into the parent's territory. Frequently, a person will report that one or both parents have died, but the connection remains intact after death until it is severed. Some people will mention that a parent, usually the mother, died at their birth or when they were very young, so that they hardly remember that parent. They were usually brought up by grandparents, other relatives, friends, in an orphanage or foster home, or by adoptive parents. In such cases, the separation front the real parents, even though they had so little influence on the child, should be undertaken first. In addition, they will need to separate from whoever reared them or had a direct influence on them during childhood.

Occasionally, we will meet someone who still has such a bitter hatred for a parent that it is too difficult or disturbing for him to visualize that parent each day. There are several ways of dealing with this problem: instead of visualizing the actual person, a picture, initials, or a symbol which represents him or her can be used.

One woman with whom my daughter was working was still so terrified of her father that she could not do the exercise at all. We asked to be shown what to tell her and it was suggested that she imagine putting up a very thick screen between herself and her father, to think of hint on the other side of this protecting wall in his own circle, separated from her. She agreed to try this and found that it was then possible for her to practise the Figure Eight as required in preparation to free herself from his influence. This woman had been used incestuously by her father from a very early age and was still suffering from the effects by repeated failures to sustain a lasting relationship with a man. We have found that incest is far more common than is generally recognized. We have been given various ways of helping with this problem, which I will describe in a later chapter.

The majority of people are usually able to visualize and, with practice, this ability quickly improves, but there are always a few who find it difficult and even impossible. For these we have several alternative ways of beaming the symbol to their subconscious and sometimes they themselves will be able to come up with a way to solve this difficulty. I recall one young woman who drew a large diagram of a Figure Eight on paper with the help of a compass and, with a pale blue crayon, outlined it several times each morning and evening.

Many people find that during spare moments, such as while waiting for an appointment, they catch themselves doodling, so we often suggest that they keep a small pad and pencil at hand whenever possible on which they can doodle the Figure Eight while they wait, putting the initials of themselves and the parent in the middle of each circle. One man cut two circles out of paper which he placed on the floor of his room, sat in one and put a picture of his mother in the other, and proceeded to trace around the Figure Eight, with his finger, and imagine the glow of blue light.

This gave me an idea for another woman who had been given the Figure Eight to visualize before detaching, not from a parent but from her husband, whom she was in the process of divorcing. She was very nervous and found it difficult to concentrate so I suggested that she cut out the two circles and place them on the floor, and then actually walk around the outline of the Figure Eight. She found that she could easily follow this suggestion and the physical activity drained off some of her nervous energy which had prevented her from being able to concentrate. Incidentally, this is a typical example of how we are often shown a technique while working with one person which can be used for others with a similar problem.

After carefully explaining the Figure Eight, we watch as the person describes how he is going to do it to be sure he has understood and is visualizing it correctly. I would like to stress the importance of checking in this way as we have had many experiences when we thought we had made it clear only to discover that the person was drawing the symbol not on the ground around his feet, but in the air around his waist, chest or neck and sometimes above his head. Others were seeing it in a vertical position with the circles one on top of the other. Misunderstandings like these seem to occur more often if the exercise is given over the telephone, which we prefer not to do except in an emergency when there is an urgent need for someone to start using it as soon as possible. The best way to avoid confusion is to have the person repeat the directions aloud so that they can be checked and any questions may be asked.

In addition to the Figure Eight, there are two other activities which should be started at the same time. We ask the person to log his dreams and make it a habit to write them down each morning or as soon as he awakens from a dream and can still remember it. Most people have had the experience of waking up with a dream still vivid in their mind, perhaps even being able to analyze it immediately, and then being so certain that it is too clear to be forgotten, they go back to sleep only to awaken in the morning unabled to remember anything but the fact that they dreamed. To avoid losing dreams in this way and with them, possible important messages from the subconscious, we suggest having a pad and pencil, or a tape recorder near the bed to make it a simple matter to record a dream as soon as it is recalled. We also suggest that as a person prepares for sleep, the subconscious should be directed to give him a dream that will instruct him in whatever way would be helpful at that particular time. A dream can very often indicate the main problem in a person's life and so cut down the time otherwise used to uncover the clue to his difficulties.

We also suggest that he start to compile lists of his parents' positive and negative attributes to help him see more clearly how he was programmed by them during childhood and how he reacted to his parents by conforming or rebelling. We suggest taking two large sheets of paper, one for each parent, and drawing a line down the middle of each to make two columns. On the left hand side of each page should be written that parent's characteristics or habits to which he reacted negatively, and on the right hand side all the traits to which he reacted positively or admired. These lists take time and patience and should not be hurried or even finished at one sitting. The most obvious insights usually come to mind immediately, but it is the small subtle ones which often make the most impression on children and are often forgotten or suppressed and which surface from the subconscious more slowly once the more striking ones have been noted. It is helpful to have a pad and pencil handy whenever possible on which to jot down the positive and negative reactions as they come to mind, for as soon as this process is started and the subconscious becomes aware of what is needed, it pulls out of the past the suppressed and forgotten reactions from childhood. This may seem like a lot to ask a person to do, but we have observed that those who are willing to work hard and are the most disciplined are the ones who have been desperate, disillusioned and dissatisfied before they came for help. This appears to be a rule.

We are all a little lazy and rarely put in real effort unless something forces us to or unless we are hurting badly enough to be willing to do almost anything to ease the pain, whether the cause is physical, mental, emotional, financial, or strong enough in whatever way to galvanize us into action. There are, of course those who are so inspired by the adventure of the work that this in itself motivates them; for it is emotional energy that makes it possible for a person to break through the barrier put up by the conscious mind and make contact with the subconscious.

Another interesting occurrence observed over the years is that in many cases a person asking to work either cannot arrange to start immediately or is unable to keep the first appointment. Instead of adding frustration to a person already feeling insecure, it has become apparent that, instead, the delay makes most people even more anxious to start and helps to build up more energy with which to make the first breakthrough, which is so important.

Chapter 4

# PUBERTY RITE —
# CUTTING THE TIES
# TO ONE PARENT

In order to enter a state of inner awareness, it is first necessary for the physical body to be as relaxed as possible to reduce to a minimum the possibility of discomfort or distraction from tension in muscles or nerves. A relaxation routine has gradually evolved after working with many people, and the duration has been set with the average person in mind. Particularly tense people may need to pay extra attention to certain parts of the body where we all carry tension, such as the back of the neck and shoulders. At the end of the primary relaxation, these parts of the body can be given further suggestions until the person reports that his entire body is relaxed. It is wise to suggest a visit to the toilet before starting the relaxation to forestall the need to break off during the session, since strong emotions usually affect the bladder. However, it should be stressed that it is advisable for the person to get up whenever necessary rather than be distracted by the discomfort of a full bladder. With practice, it is possible to get up, visit the bathroom, return and slip right back into the same state without a break in the inner experience. Neckties, belts, bras, should be loosened or removed, shoes should be taken off and any jewellery which might be distracting should be put somewhere safe.

The person about to enter the waking dream state is then asked whether a prone or sitting position is generally more conducive to relaxation, and it is explained that the goal is to relax the body as completely as possible so that it does not distract in any way from the experience of the waking dream. Some people associate the prone position with sleep, in which case it would be preferable for them to sit upright, or recline slightly. A lightweight blanket or cover should be provided, as most people tend to feel chilly when deeply relaxed and, if the prone position is preferred, a pillow should be offered.

As soon as the person is sitting or lying comfortably, a light scarf is tied loosely around his head to cover the eyes so that any pictures seen will be clearer and to give a sense of partial privacy in the event that strong emotions may be aroused.

We have found that some people prefer to go mentally to an imaginary or favourite place, while others feel perfectly content to be where they are physically. So we suggest various possibilities to help the person to decide, such as a shady wood, the top of a hill, under the sheltering branches of a big old tree, lying in a swing or hammock, in a cave, in one's own bedroom. We next ask the person to state his preferred place and we suggest that he go to that scene in imagination and become comfortable, letting go, wriggling the feet, buttocks and shoulders, moving the head about, and dropping the arms limply at either side of the body.

Then we explain that we have been taught to use either sunlight or moonlight to relax and fill the body to protect it while we work and give it a healing treatment. The subject is asked for his preference. Most people hardly hesitate at all and frequently the scene that they have chosen in imagination helps them to decide on the type of light. When the person has made his choice, we explain that verbal instructions will be given to various parts of the body to open up and receive the light. However, we do not want to assume any control over anyones mind or body, so the person is asked to repeat the suggestions silently to his own body.

We then explain that the light has, for our work, four properties: it is relaxing, healing, cleansing and regenerating or re-energizing.

We also explain that these four qualities will be repeated verbally quite often during the relaxation so that the suggestions will be impressed on the subconscious mind and allowed to take effect, as the subconscious thrives on repetition.

It is useful to have a tape recording of the relaxation technique so that people can use it at home to practise relaxing on their own. This cuts down the time taken for relaxation at the beginning of each session. A tape can be made of the person's own voice or that of anyone relaxing him. Eventually, most people find that they can slip into this relaxed state quite quickly and with very little help after the first few times. Another benefit of using a tape is that the person can use it at home when he is tense or tired or when he finds it is difficult to relax sufficiently to fall asleep.

I will present the relaxation suggestions verbatim, as if I were actually working with someone.

### Relaxation Suggestions

"Imagine that you are making yourself as comfortable as possible in the place you have chosen in your mind for this session and, when you are settled, tell me where you are in your inner scene.

As I have explained to you, we use either sunlight or moonlight in this relaxing treatment, so tell me whether it is night-time or daytime so that I will know which to use.

I will give you verbal directions to help you to relax, but I do not wish to control either your body or your mind in any way, so please repeat the directions to the various parts of your body after me. I mention them so that your body obeys *your* orders, not mine.

Visualize a ray of light shining down onto you and direct it to your toes. Let go of your toes as much as possible, and give the order that they open up to receive the light which has, for our purpose, four attributes: relaxing, healing, cleansing and re-energizing. I shall repeat these four several times during the relaxation in order to impress them on your subconscious mind, which needs repetition in order to accept the message and put it into effect.

Feel the light enter your toes in a warm soothing stream and gradually move up over your insteps, the soles of your feet, around your heels and up into your ankles, so that your feet are now filled with light in every muscle, bone, nerve and cell. Now watch as it moves up your lower legs into your calves, and on up to the knees. Give the order to your lower legs to receive the light, and begin to feel it penetrating every bone, muscle, nerve and cell, relaxing, healing, cleansing and re-energizing wherever needed.

Now direct your upper legs to open up to receive this soothing flow of light, watching as it moves past your knees and up into your thighs, to your hips, bringing relaxation, healing, cleansing and re-energizing as needed. Now let go of your legs, thank them for carrying you around every day and give them permission to take a complete rest while taking this treatment as you will not need to use them during the coming session.

Now move your attention away from your legs and into the pelvic area, giving the order for that part of your body to receive healing. relaxing, cleansing and re-energizing of every organ, gland, nerve, muscle, as needed, all the way back to the lower part of your spine. penetrating each vertebra in that area.

Now let go of that part of your body and open up the next segment to the relaxing, healing, cleansing and re-energizing light. This includes the stomach and intestines, so feel the light flowing in and around every muscle, organ, gland and into the part of your spine at the back of the abdominal section of your body.

Now move your attention up to the solar plexus, in the middle of your body, just below your ribs. As this is the centre of your nervous system, sometimes called the secondary brain, it is most important to bring the light fully into this area, to relax, heal, cleanse and re-energize your whole nervous system, and thus reach every nerve throughout your body.

At this point I would like you to tell me what kind of flower you can see at the solar plexus. Tell me what comes first to your mind or inner vision. Do not worry if you do not know its name, merely describe it. Is this flower open or closed? If it is still closed, give the order that it open sufficiently for the light to penetrate the centre of it, and tell me when this has happened. Now direct the light into the very centre of your flower with the order that it flow to every nerve in your body, bringing with it healing, relaxing, cleansing and re-energizing. Now direct the light to penetrate all parts of this section of your body and back into the spine.

Now visualize the light moving up into the upper part of your torso, into the chest and upper back. To this area, give the order that each time you inhale you will be drawing in more light to circulate throughout your body and, as you exhale, that you will expel anything of a negative nature, such as fear, anxiety, tension, or anything else which could obstruct the flow of light. Have this order remain in effect the entire time we are working today so that your natural breathing will be helping with this treatment. Now direct the light into all parts of your upper torso and into every organ and gland, and to the spine, to bring healing, relaxing, cleansing and re-energizing where necessary.

Now visualize the light flowing down both of your arms from the shoulders, and feel it beginning to fill in the fingers, palms of your hands and your wrists, re-energizing and bringing healing, cleansing and relaxation. Now watch as the light fills in the forearms from the wrists to the elbows, penetrating every bone, muscle, nerve and cell in both of them, re-energizing and bringing relaxa-tion, healing and cleansing. Observe the light streaming into both of the upper arms, to relax, heal, cleanse and re-energize along the way. Let go of both of your arms and thank them for working for you and give them permission to take rest while we work.

Move your attention away from the arms and into your throat. Here again, we use a flower to help the treatment, as this is the entry to your glandular system. Describe the flower you see at your throat and tell me if it is open or closed. If it is closed, give the order that it open sufficiently to allow the light to enter and to stream into every gland in your body, bringing to each relaxation, healing, cleansing and re-energizing, wherever needed. Tell me when this has taken place.

Now feel the light flowing around to the back of your neck, which is where most people carry tension, and feel as if fingers of light are gently, but firmly, massaging all the muscles in your neck and shoulders, erasing any tension which is present and tell me when you feel this has been done.

Now send the light in a stream down your spine, from the back of your neck all the way down to your coccyx, or tail bone, visualizing the light flowing around each vertebra along the way, healing, relaxing, cleansing and re-energizing where needed.

Now bring the light up into your head and face, and direct it to your chin and jaws. If your tongue is up on the roof of your mouth, let it drop, and if your teeth are closed tightly together, release them to allow your jaw to relax as well as your throat so that the light can take over. Now visualize the light penetrating your cheeks, up into your ears, across to your nose, and up into your eyes, bringing to all these parts relaxation, healing, cleansing and re-energizing where needed.

Now let go of your five senses of touch, hearing, sight, smell and taste, thank them for serving you and give them rest while we work today as you will not need your physical senses for this inner work.

Now direct the light to your temples and forehead, up over your head, and deep into your brain, irradiating every part, both conscious and unconscious, and bringing relaxation, healing, cleansing and re-energizing where any of these is needed.

Now take three very deep, slow breaths, breathing in even more light with each one, and let go of any remaining tensions as you breathe out. In a very slow and lazy manner, run your inner gaze over your whole body and tell me if it is relaxed, or if there are any areas which need more attention. If you find some, simply direct the light to that particular part, with the suggestion that it relax more and more while we work.

If, for any reason, you notice tension building up in any part of your body during the time we are working, tell me as soon as you are aware of it as it may indicate a psychosomatic condition related to what you are experiencing at the time. We can then immediately seek the cause and the best way to deal with it. Frequently, just seeing the connection between what is going on in your body and what you are experiencing inside your own head will bring about a release from the physical symptom."

## Puberty Rites

After the person is relaxed, I suggest that we both imagine a triangle erected between us, explaining its function if that has not already been done. I have the person take a place at point B on the base, with me at the other end at point A, joined by a line representing the mutual trust we have for each other as working partners. Then we both visualize an antenna reaching up our spines, out from the top of each of our heads, meeting at a point in space at the apex of the triangle, which we call the High C, High Consciousness or God-self. The High C is the innate wisdom within all of us, where we are all one.

We then take time to ask that each of us be guided from that mutual High C, so that the right questions and directions will come to the one who is directing and that the person in the relaxed state will receive and be ready to handle whatever he needs to see, feel, know or experience at that particular time.

.This method has proved to be foolproof over the years and we have never had occasion when someone with whom we were working got out of his depth, or was faced with any memory, fault or old trauma that was too much for him to handle.

I then explain that the person is not to worry if this first time he sees nothing, as in that event I can easily slip into the reverie state myself and describe what I see, and then direct him according to how I am guided from within. Even if that is difficult, I make it clear that I can, if so directed, take over, watch and describe the impressions I am receiving and do whatever I am prompted to do to help on his inner level. This seems to take all the anxiety and pressure off those who may be worried that they will not be able to visualize.

Next, I ask the person to visualize the two circles of the Figure Eight which are already familiar from the two-week daily practice periods, and then invite into the circle opposite the one he is in the parent from whom he is about to separate. I tell him to explain to the parent that the ritual about to be performed will free both of them so that each will be able to live his own life as a separate individual and will no longer be pulled this way and that by the actions of the other via the cords which still bind them together. I then encourage the person to see if he can see the ties between him and his parent, and to tell me at which parts of the body on each person the cords are attached. Most people seem to be able to visualize this fairly easily and some are really shocked at what they see. I warn the person not to be disturbed since what he sees will show us how best to help the relationship.

It is not at all unusual for the parent of the opposite sex to be joined to the child between the sex organs, telling us a great deal about their relationship and showing us where they will need to work if they ever hope to have a good relationship with someone of the opposite sex.

Some people find only one link while others discover several, depending on the closeness, either positive or negative, of the relationship. We have had a few cases where the connection was so strong that the two were like Siamese twins. In these situations, it was impossible for the person desiring to be free to see clearly and it was out of the question to expect him to perform the 'surgery' himself. In this case the person directing the session must be willing to perform the operation for him, urging him to participate as much as possible.

When the ties have been located, I ask for a description of the size and texture and, here again, I have heard literally hundreds of different descriptions, all symbolic of the relationship and often astonishingly revealing. There have been velvet ribbons, nylon thread, fishing lines, wire, rope chains, metal bars, and many, many other types of cords.

When the nature of the ties has been determined, I tell him to ask to be shown the appropriate instrument with which to sever or detach the bonds, and again the selection is surprisingly varied. Scissors, all kinds of knives such as kitchen and hunting knives, swords, and daggers, light rays, laser beams, fire, acid, saws, to mention but a few, are forthcoming.

I usually suggest that the first cut be made in the middle of the bond and then each end removed from each person's body where it is attached. Frequently, I have to help remove the end from the person doing the detaching if it happens to be on a part of the body which is hard for him to reach or is too sensitive for him to dare to tackle on his own with any confidence of success.

As each end is removed, I suggest placing the right hand (if the person is right handed, otherwise the left hand) over the place where it was removed on either body, with the other hand behind it to create a force field. Then we ask that a healing force flow down from the High C into his hands and into the wound left by the cutting.

The ties are then placed in a pile at the feet of the person working and, when they have all been detached, he asks to be shown the best method of destroying them, thus preventing them from returning to continue the old pattern.

Most people choose to burn or bury, dissolve with acid, or hurl the bonds into the sea or a fast-flowing river. Frequently, people are so anxious to be finished with such ties that they cannot think of enough to do to be sure they are definitely destroyed, often deciding to bury the fire in which they have burned them and then jumping up and down on the site to erase all evidence of it. This has, at times, developed into something like an Indian war dance. which! then suggest should become an expression of the person's relief at being finally free. I encourage them to let go and express this freedom in any way they choose.

After they are satisfied that everything has been done to erase all trace of the old ties. I suggest they thank the parent from whom they have just been separated for providing the means for them to enter the world in a human body. and thus be able to learn whatever was necessary in this life.

Next the person performs a ritual in which he asks forgiveness from the parent and forgives the parent for any hurts that have been inflicted on him, consciously or unconsciously. This is often very hard for the person to do, especially in a case where there are hard feelings between him and the parent. It is essential that the forgiving be done as it is part of the process of becoming detached and whole. Lack of forgiveness can forge the links all over again in a negative way.

I usually start by having the person first ask the parent for forgiveness, as this part of the ritual seems to be, for most people, slightly easier: many people suffer from a load of guilt and this presents the person with an opportunity to relieve himself of the burden. I suggest that he allow specific things to come to mind for which he would like forgiveness and either to verbalize them or silently mention them, one at a time. If he chooses to be silent. I ask him to let me know when he has finished, to the best of his knowledge. I also tell him that anything more coming up later can always be handled at that time. We find that this opportunity to ask forgiveness is most welcome and frees the person from the haunting sense of guilt and regret which people are so often left with, particularly after the parent has passed on.

The next step is to forgive the parent for any hurts or wrongs inflicted, either consciously or unconsciously on the one seeking release. This is by far the harder task for most people and, in some cases, they find it impossible to attempt.

At such times. I suggest that even though the person cannot find it in his heart to forgive this parent, he can ask the High C, or God-force within him, to send forgiveness from the top of the triangle between us down through himself and across to the parent. This is almost always acceptable even by those who know they need to forgive but cannot bring themselves to do so on their own. Again, I suggest that they allow specific episodes to enter their minds where forgiveness of the parent is needed to set them both free from the negative emotions which bind people just as strongly as positive ones.

Finally, the parent is asked to leave the scene and go on his way to lead his own life, now free from the constant emotional tug of the child. This request does not necessarily mean that there will be no further contact between them; indeed, most people find that, on the contrary, the relationship becomes much less emotionally charged and more satisfactory.

We always suggest an appropriate parting, preferably with a blessing. Sometimes it is indicated that a triangle be visualized between the parent and child connecting them both to the High C instead of to one another. We have been shown that this visualization is the most helpful thing anyone can do for another person, and we call it running the triangle'. We often do this ourselves when we receive a call for help (even before the person has been told anything about it) to connect him to the High C as quickly as possible.

One further step is taken to complete the release. This is a cleansing process, which is designed to wash away all old conditioning and habit patterns. This process is a preparation for working on habits separately, which will be discussed in the next chapter. Sometimes the release is immediate, but it can also take a longer time to become evident.

I usually suggest that the person look around his inner scene for a body of water, such as a stream, pool, ocean, or waterfall. He is then instructed to remove all his clothes, to leave them in a pile on the ground and, taking a large leaf or smooth stone, to enter the water and wash himself thoroughly. This will remove unwanted negative habit patterns or attitudes picked up from parents, and he should recall them from the lists he has already compiled of his parents' negative attributes. When he is satisfied that he has cleansed himself of them, he is told to run up and down to dry himself off, jumping and leaping to express his freedom. When he is dry, I hand him a fresh loose robe or gown of a neutral colour to wear until he grows a new set of attributes of his own, or, if prompted from within, I lead him to find his own new garment. Then I ask how he would like to destroy the old clothing which ties him to his childhood reactions. Most often he will decide to burn his old clothes and, as in every other part of the work, I am often amazed at some of the elaborate methods people will choose to destroy them.

The most important part of the work is the person's own active participation, which alone can reach through to the subconscious mind. The more emotion involved, the deeper the subconscious is impressed with the new message, and thus, the sooner the message will be put into effect. Most people are delighted at the opportunity to rid themselves of their old unwanted habits and find no problem becoming emotionally involved in the process.

I always warn the person that for the next three days after the session he can expect to experience mixed emotions, such as mourning or sadness mixed with relief, but that he need not worry as this is quite usual and will soon pass. If the warning is not given, and the person does go into a depression or some similar change or mood, it may come as a shock and throw doubt on the whole experience.

It is also advisable to tell the person not to talk about his experience with anyone for at least three days, as the emotional energy needs to be contained to give it a chance to stabilize, solidify and become a reality. Talking about it too soon can allow the energy to leak away, especially if the person to whom the experience is described happens to be sceptical and expresses doubt. This reaction is infectious and becomes like a blight on the still delicate new growth within the person who has just worked.

We then both thank the High C for directing the session and I give verbal suggestions to bring the person back to full awareness of his physical body, which I remind him has been given a healing treatment during the time we were working on the inner level. I suggest that he wriggle his toes, bend his knees, move his hips, arch his back, and stretch his arms, all reminiscent of a dog or cat stretching the whole body upon awakening from sleep.

I then emphasize the day's date and that he is in my workroom and that he can now sit up slowly, remove the scarf from his eyes, return to full conscious awareness, and begin to function freely after his recent release.

Then I explain that it is advisable after cutting the ties, particularly those connected to parents, to write an unmailed letter to the parent expressing his release. This letter bypasses the conscious mind of the person to whom it is addressed but reaches his subconscious. It is best written as soon after the cutting ceremony as possible when strong emotions aroused by the ritual are usually still present. The more emotion with which the letter is written, the deeper the effect it will have on both the one writing it and on the one to whom it is addressed, since emotion is the energy which is needed to carry the message to the subconscious level of the mind. The letter should be a repetition of the statement made during the ritual that each person is now free to live as a separate individual. It should not include anything negative, such as criticism or blame, and should concentrate only on the freedom both will now begin to experience. I have seen some dramatic results when this has been done with strong emotion.

I recall one case where a son who had had no contact with his parents for several years, suddenly and without knowing the reason, called them long distance on the phone after his mother had gone through the ceremony of cutting the tight connection which she had seen still existed between them, and had written the follow-up unmailed letter.

Another young man, also without knowing why he was doing it, called to tell his parents that he loved them. He had never been able to say this before. This occurred after his father had detached cords from him and set him free to live his own life.

There are many cases of parents changing their old attitudes to their grown children when the latter have cut the binding ties. Their reports always refer to a cessation of tension and to a more flowing relationship. In addition to this easing of tension, people mention that it has become much easier to talk than ever before and to see one another for the first time as people and not just as relatives.

If the person has been reared by people other than the natural parents, he should be helped to release from these after cutting the ties to his-own parents. The method is almost identical to that described above except that, instead of thanking the parents for supplying entry into a physical body, it is more appropriate to thank them for assuming the responsibility for his care in place of his parents. For other members of the family who have had partial influence on the growing child such as grandparents, the wording of the ceremony can be adjusted and adapted appropriately.

# Chapter 5

# DEALING WITH NEGATIVE PARENTAL ARCHETYPES

As I have already mentioned, in order for a person over the age of puberty to be free to develop as an independent individual, it is necessary for him to release from both parents, whether they happen to have had a good or negative influence on the child in question, whatever his age.

However, in the case of negative parents, a further step is necessary as, invariably, such a parent has assumed archetypal or larger-than-life proportions in the eyes of the child. The archetype also has to be dealt with. In such cases, there are two distinct rituals: one to free the child from the negative mother and the other to release him from the negative father. To facilitate this, symbolic personifications have been given to us, such as dragons, witches, giants and ogres from fairy tales and black widow spiders, octopuses, and assorted monsters.

After the relaxation has been completed and the triangle erected, we suggest that the person ask his High C to show him a figure which, for him, will represent the negative parent archetype overshadowing him. I will describe a typical experience of my own in dealing with an overpoweringly negative mother.

When I had been using the reverie technique to work on myself for a comparatively short time I experienced a typical confrontation with the dragon which, for me, represented the negative mother archetype. At the time, I only dimly comprehended the significance of what was happening. It was not until later, when we were shown other symbolic figures and their meaning was explained, that we realized that we were being shown a method by which people could be helped to free themselves from such powerful forces.

As soon as I had relaxed into the waking dream state, I became aware that I was riding a horse and was clad in a suit of armour like the knights of old. Soon it became clear to me that I was bound on an inner adventure and was on my way to kill a dragon which was devouring people at an alarming rate. I instinctively knew that I must take the dragon unawares, so I dismounted from my horse, tied him to a nearby tree and proceeded on foot towards a cave in which I felt sure the dragon was hiding. With my shield held in front of me with my left hand, and my spear in my right hand, I made my way stealthily towards the cave where I could see the dragon lying asleep. I knew I must find the vulnerable spot under its belly over the heart and pierce it with my spear. As it had been taken by surprise, I had the advantage and, after a short bout with it, my spear entered its soft belly from which gushed blood as it snorted and lashed its tail in its death throes. I watched until all of its blood had flowed out and seeped into the earth on which it was lying, realizing that the blood would fertilize the earth and ensure that the new growth would be strong and plentiful. As soon as I was sure that this had taken place and no further movements or sounds were coming from the dragon, I moved over and stood on its back with the spear held high over my head in triumph. I was all alone, no one was there to see me and I knew that this was an inner victory. I became aware that the spear was burning my hand as it was still coated with blood. I pushed the helmet back from my face and held the bloody spear high as an offering to God, feeling a wonderful sense of exhilaration at the success of triumphing over the dragon.

There I stood for some minutes, with my feet braced against the back of the dragon, pressing them down so that I could feel the scales, looking flamboyant but feeling not the least bit egotistical, just profoundly thankful that the dragon lay dead under my feet with its blood fertilizing the earth. I was filled with awe. I knelt down beside the carcass, thrust the spear through the body which was now just a shell, took off my helmet and hung it on top of the spear. I removed my armour and draped it around the spear and, using this as an altar, I knelt down humbly to give thanks that there was nothing more to fear.

As I started to get up I saw, emerging from the back of the cave, an old bent crone who, as soon as she saw me and the dead dragon, suddenly straightened up and, as she did so her skin, formerly wrinkled and dry, crumpled and cracked and began to fall off revealing a beautiful young girl.

There was a river nearby with a small waterfall, so we both went hand in hand to wash ourselves in the clear cool water. She cleansed herself from the remains of the old skin and I washed off the blood of the dragon so that we were both made new. Now that we had found each other, we could go together on the path up the mountain to become one with the High C.

We have conducted many people through similar rituals. Some used a dragon, while others were shown different symbols for the overpowering negative mother such as an old witch, an octopus, a black widow spider and other mythical she-monsters.

The important task to be accomplished by both men and women is to free the feminine part of themselves which has been imprisoned by a dominating negative mother archetype. The pattern for the feminine nature is usually set by the mother and the masculine pattern by the father. If either part has been smothered or over-powered by a strong parent, the person is out of balance, with one aspect strong and other weak.

After such a session, the relief is sometimes so great that it is unbelievable to the person experiencing it. Often a flood of tears will erupt, releasing the pocket of negative energy which had been buried inside for so long. An interesting result of this release is that the natural mother and her influence usually shrink down to normal size and become much easier to deal with.

As in other separations, we warn the person that the three days following the session may be emotionally charged but that he need not let this worry him as the mood will fade. He will then experience a new sense of freedom and an influx of energy which has been walled off in the negative figure and is now free to be used.

When a man is taken through the release from the devouring or smothering negative mother, his own anima, or feminine feeling aspect, is freed from bondage and becomes available to function more fully and effectively in his daily life. When a woman is taken through the battle with the negative mother, her own animus, or masculine aspect, is called upon to engage the monster in battle. I have used the terms anima and animus which Carl Jung used to designate the female part of a man and the male part of a woman. These terms will be discussed in more detail in a later chapter. With the help of the animus, the female subject is able to free her own feminine nature which had been overshadowed since childhood.

The overshadowing negative father is usually symbolized by a giant or ogre, and most often by a one-eyed cyclops. It is imperative that the person seeking release from this force should prepare very carefully for the confrontation. He should put on a protective suit of armour, mount a horse and take in his hand a sword, dagger or other appropriate weapon with which to perform the ritual killing. The negative father archetype must be approached very quietly and under cover of darkness while he is asleep lest he attack first. There is one vulnerable spot at which to aim the weapon, just as there was in the dragon. In the case of a cyclops, his single eye must first be put out. He can then more easily be killed by a thrust of the knife into his heart. As soon as he is dead the male figure who has been imprisoned either inside him or in his castle or tower must be freed from incarceration and reunited with his rescuer.

The result of this reunion is equally helpful for a man or a woman. As with the release from the negative mother, it leads to the possibility of a balance between the male and female aspects of the person. The variations on the above themes are limitless, though the main outline is invariably quite similar from person to person. The details often vary according to the images each person brings to the session from his past experiences and his ability to visualize.

The benefits resulting from release from these two negative archetypes are of equal value for both men and women. When a person of either sex is free from their influence both the feeling and thinking functions associated with the anima and animus can be brought into better balance. It will then be possible for the person to become more whole by using both aspects instead of leaning on another person to supply the missing one.

Chapter 6

# POSTIVE AND NEGATIVE ATTRIBUTES OF PARENTS

As soon as a release from the parents has been achieved, it is essential to look at them as people and as impersonally as possible in order to determine the extent to which their child was programmed by them, either consciously or unconsciously.

Early programming is of two kinds: direct teaching and influence by example. But these do not always match as it is easy to tell someone else what to do and what is right or wrong, but very difficult to put these same theories into daily practice. We are all hypocrites to some degree and fall short of practising what we preach, however hard we try and protest to the contrary.

However, it is not the actions of the parents or their teaching as such that affect us either benignly or adversely, but the different ways we reacted to their behaviour and treatment of us. We either copied them or rebelled against them and, as neither of these alternatives allows the true self to be expressed, it is very important to see these reactions clearly and to try to understand them in order to discover who we really are beneath the false front of borrowed attitudes. Only then can we consciously decide which attributes are valuable and should be kept, and which should be abandoned.

Reactions lead directly to value judgments: we either like or dislike what we see or experience. If we are strictly honest with ourselves, we must agree that when we criticize someone with strong emotional intensity, one of two alternatives is operating. Our criticisms of others can be projections of our own faults of which we are unaware. It is much easier to criticize someone else for being selfish, dishonest, rude or egotistical than to admit to these same faults in ourselves. The more emotional we are in our criticisms, the more likely we are to be guilty of those same faults or failings. The reason for this is that we are too close to our own weaknesses and either too short-sighted or too lazy to admit to and correct them.

But there is another hidden and rather subtle reason for criticizing others which is often overlooked. Those actions or traits which we object to in others may be exaggerated examples of the very qualities which we lack and need to develop in ourselves to bring about a better balance, but which we are either too fearful of or too inhibited to express. We feel guilty and inadequate so we criticize those who are free to express themselves in a particular way, though often too blatantly, rather than developing those qualities ourselves to bring about a better balance. For instance, often a very shy person will ridicule someone who is very outgoing and aggressive rather than use the person as a mirror to help to reveal a lack which he needs to be made aware of so that he can consciously work on it. In such cases the criticism masks an underlying jealousy and feeling of inadequacy.

As long as we continue to act in either of these ways, we can never know who we really are beneath the reactions. Only when we are willing to use everyone we meet as mirrors in which to catch glimpses of ourselves can we begin to let down our defenses and look within to discover what we are really like.

As our parents were our first mirrors, we must look at them objectively to see where we have imitated those qualities we admire in them and where we rebelled against those we disliked and vowed never to repeat ourselves. These two reactions can force us to extremes, our true selves lying somewhere in between. As we become more aware of our reactions to our parents and the reasons for them, we can start making conscious decisions to change the qualities in us that we dislike in our parents instead of trying to change our parents. This is why we ask a person to compile the lists of attributes which can be used to help him towards greater self-awareness.

The first step is to mark those traits which evoke a strong emotional reaction, for those will be the very ones that can be used to turn the critical gaze inward in search of their counterpart within. Where have we copied and where have we rebelled? What is our real attitude or opinion now that we are no longer children and have finally detached ourselves from our parents and their early conditioning of us? If such questions are asked sincerely and with a genuine desire to become whole, glimpses of unrecognized or hidden aspects will be brought up into consciousness for inspection, which can lead the way to correction or modification.

It is best to take one negative attribute at a time and make it a practice to become aware of it in our own behaviour during the day, catching sight of instances or situations where it shows itself as an undesirable and unwanted trait limiting our growth. As soon as it is recognized, it can be worked on and relinquished. If, on the other hand, we become aware of the lack of a particular quality which we criticize in others, then obviously this can point the way towards working on developing this weak area.

One excellent way to facilitate the process of working on the tendencies which we would like to eradicate was given several years ago when my daughter and I first started to work on a fairly regular basis, long before she became a psychologist. During one of our sessions she was told to buy a package of mixed coloured cards. Each time a fault was pointed out to her as we worked, or when she became aware of one herself and was willing to release from it, she was told to choose a card of a specific colour and write on it daily for a week all the episodes during each day which made her aware of this weakness in herself, as well as the circumstances which brought it to her attention. Thus anger could be recorded on a red card, jealousy on a yellow one, laziness on green, dishonesty on blue, greed on beige, and so on. She found that this method helped her to become aware of areas which needed attention in a way that presented her with a challenge, since she could see for herself how well she was progressing when she reviewed what she had written on the cards from day to day.

It helps greatly for a person to discuss regularly with a counsellor the contents of the cards. This will help to clarify the underlying causes for a particular habit which, in turn, leads to ways of handling it. This method hastens the process of shedding aspects of ourselves which hinder our progress. Very often a dream will occur at the prefect time to give further insights. Included in the dream will be a person who exhibits one of the dreamer's faults, but in an exaggerated form which makes it easier to recognize. Thus, the character in the dream can, in the same way as live people, act as a mirror to reflect the fault for the dreamer to see more clearly. Once seen and recognized as blocks to further growth, many ways can be found to eradicate unwanted traits by sending a message to that effect to the subconscious.

We have been given special visualization exercises to flash to the subconscious part of the mind which will be listed in the chapter on symbols. Until we decide to work on them, the hidden parts within us keep us in a state of constant conflict and prevent us from becoming fully conscious and whole, that is, with no unknown parts pulling us away from our quest for freedom.

All of this house cleaning' is so much easier to do after a clear-cut separation from the parents has been achieved as it is then possible to gain a better perspective on our situation. It is also very important to keep in mind that the parents no longer occupy a place of authority within us and that all decisions from now on can and should be made by us with the help and direction of the High C, which alone knows best what we need at any given time.

This process is an invaluable aid to the discovery of a person's true identity and one which can help the seeker to free himself from the old conditioning which hides his real self.

"Know thyself, and the truth shall set you free."

## Destroying Negative Programming

Some people find that negative programming by parents during childhood has become so automatic, and the habit grooves have dug so deep into the nervous system, that it is extremely difficult to break them or replace them with more positive ones. Very early in the work I was brought face to face with this problem and, when I asked to be shown how I could handle it, I was given a very interesting picture to illustrate it.

I saw' a snow-covered slope on which were clearly defined ski tracks. As I looked at this scene, I realized how easy it would be to slip into those tracks and take the same route down the slope.

This explained why it is so easy to repeat an old pattern. I also knew that the fear of repeating it paralyzed me and prevented me from taking any action to change it and make a new set of tracks.

I asked to be shown what I could do to remedy this situation and the answer came flashing into my mind like a streak of lightning: 'Put on skis and slalom hack and forth across the old tracks.' In my imagination, I did exactly that and felt tremendous exhilaration to be doing something definite to cut across the old pattern. This also helped to dispel the former numbing fear and paralysis.

From then on, whenever I caught myself about to repeat an old habit, I would quickly visualize the criss-cross marks made by the skis cutting across the old tracks and then make a brand new track. This visualization exercise helped me to make a conscious decision to act in the new preferred way instead of slipping back into the old pattern again.

There have been many variations on the theme of this technique as each person found his own method for dealing with the problem. Some people find that it is helpful to write out in longhand all the old habits from which they wish to free themselves. When the list is complete it can be destroyed in any way they are shown, burning being the most common. As I was working with one young man, he took the two lists he had compiled of his parents' negative attributes and added some of his own bad habits. Then in his mind's eye, he cut the lists into strips so that each habit or tendency was on a separate piece of paper. Next, holding one piece at a time he proclaimed in a very loud and authoritative voice that he wished to let go of this particular trait and then threw it into the fire. He put a great deal of emotion into this activity and described how he poked the burning papers further into the fire to be sure that they were all destroyed completely and that no trace of them was left. He completed this ritual very quickly with obvious delight and when he had finished his task he gave an Indian war whoop to express his relief.

It is usually sufficient for a person to go through such a ritual just once a while in the waking dream state. However, sometimes a person will ask if he can repeat it at home by burning actual pieces of paper on which he has written his old negative habits. This is an excellent idea and it is most important for a person to do whatever will ensure that the message to discard his negative attitudes will reach his subconscious mind where the habits are rooted. Physical involvement of this type provides a quick and effective way to achieve this result, and is especially helpful if some negative habits had been overlooked in the first session or if the person has slipped back into the old habit grooves or patterns.

Another excellent technique requires the person to read aloud from the list of negative habits directly into a tape recorder. Many people find this to be particularly appropriate since old conditioning or programming is currently referred to as 'old tapes'. One man found that all he needed to do was to record his list of the negative ways in which he was conditioned as a child and immediately erase it. Then he recorded a new list of positive ways to replace the old ones. He would play the new tape from time to time to reaffirm his desire to change.

But not everyone finds it so simple to reverse old ways, and for some people an inner ritual is needed to impress the subconscious with the new message. I recall one woman with whom I worked who had been brought up strictly according to a rigid set of rules. It appeared that her mother had been so insecure when faced with bringing up her first child that she asked her paediatrician to give her detailed diet sheets to which she adhered to the letter. The woman had found these sheets years later tucked into her baby book. She read aloud to me directions for specific amounts of food, such as one teaspoonful of cereal, one tablespoonful of pureed fruit, one-quarter cupful of mashed potato, and so on. Then she read from the bottom of each sheet a list of absolutely forbidden foods which, of course, included all those which are favourites with young children such as ice cream, candy or desserts of any kind. I was not at all surprised that she had had a weight problem all her adult life, for she had obviously rebelled at such a strict regime and was continuing to do so by overeating.

I suggested that we both ask her High C to show us what could be done to help her, to which she eagerly agreed. As soon as we had erected the triangle, I saw her as a little girl of about a year and a half, wearing a headset with earphones like those worn in planes while watching a film. It was connected to a tape recorder and the cassette being played continuously was one of her mother's voice reading aloud from the doctor's lists as she prepared the child's meals; at the same time the mother urged her to finish everything on her plate, saying she would have to stay in her high chair until the plate was empty.

I suggested to the woman that she visualize a picture of herself as a little girl and, in her imagination, pull the earphones away from her ears and remove the headset. She could do this easily, so I suggested that she tell the child that she could do anything she wanted to destroy the headset and the cassette. She reported that when she did this the child first appeared to be frightened at such an order. I suggested that she explain to her inner child that she would take the place of her mother from now on and that she need not fear punishment for destroying the tape as they both needed to be rid of it in order to be free from the old conditioning. After quite a long pause, she reported that when the child understood, she proceeded to stamp on the tape recorder and pull out the tape which she tangled into a snarl.

When she reported that the child had done all she could to destroy it, I directed her to tell the child to gather it all up into a pile and decide how best to destroy it completely. She then described how the child pulled up the skirt of her dress, piled all the parts of the tape and headset into it, and carried them over to a fire which she could see burning brightly in a fire-place. She emptied her skirt into the fire and watched with great glee as the flames reduced everything to ashes.

I then suggested, that she tell the child to do whatever she liked to express her freedom from those old rigid rules. Immediately she described a beautiful green meadow and, as she watched, the little girl ran into it and started to dance and twirl, laughing delightedly at being free. When she told me that the child was lying down in the grass, rolling over in sheer delight, I suggested that she join her to share her enjoyment.

While they relaxed in the cool grass, we discussed some practical aids, such as the best hours during the day to eat each of three meals, which foods should be avoided for a while and which could be eaten. At the same time I urged her to provide herself with a wide choice. Then I asked her which items were her biggest temptations. She replied without a moment's hesitation, "Ice cream", which of course was one of the first items on the list of don'ts' in her baby schedule. I suggested that she explain to her inner little girl that from now on she would be taking the place of her mother, and that she would be responsible for her own welfare, but that there would be a few rules which must be kept until new habits had been learned. However, once a week on the same day and at a specific time, they would have a treat, which could be ice cream or anything else she might be craving at that time.

This method can be applied to any habit or appetite and varied as each person seeks help with his particular problem. These few examples can be used as suggestions to help people to discover their own ways of dealing with 'old tapes'. However, whatever the method chosen, it should be dramatic enough and acted out with sufficient emotion to reach the subconscious so that it can proceed to put the suggestion into effect.

Chapter 7

# CONNECTING TO INNER COSMIC PARENTS

## The Tree

The tree has been given as a symbol of the impersonal Self, which is beyond the opposites and therefore so secure that none of the joys or sorrows of life can affect it. It is rooted in the earth or the Cosmic Mother and reaches up to the sun or the Cosmic Father, drawing its sustenance from both these sources in order to stand firm and upright between heaven and earth.

We use this symbol in an exercise to help people prepare for the eventual attainment of freedom from the constant pull of the opposites. It also links people to their own versions of the Cosmic Mother and Father, archetypes we all share and which contain the real nourishment we all need but rarely receive from our own parents, however loving and helpful they have tried to be. In certain cases when a person feels extreme insecurity at the thought of detaching from his parents, we give him an exercise using the tree before the puberty rites. We also prescribe it after he cuts the cords to his parents, so that when he is detached from their binding influence he may immediately make a link with the Cosmic Parents who are common to all of us and uniquely capable of sustaining us.

We find that people who use the tree symbol diligently gradually become aware of an increased sense of security, well-being and strength, and the persistent feeling of rejection or lack of love, which have so often haunted them since childhood, fade away.

A young man to whom I had given this exercise, following a successful detachment from his mother, telephoned me and excitedly told me that he felt more sure of himself than he could ever remember feeling in his whole life. He finally exclaimed, 'It's sheer magic!', to which I replied, "Only when you yourself practise it, for that's the secret of the success of these symbols."

It is of little use for someone merely to describe the symbols to people, for though they hear the description it reaches only the conscious mind, which may react to it either favourably or negatively and often forgets it immediately. It is essential that the technique be practised daily by the person himself, to imprint the symbol on his subconscious mind, for only then will it be effective in his daily life.

I will now give instructions for the tree exercise, which can be varied slightly from person to person:

"Close your eyes and relax and withdraw into an inner scene. Ask your High C to select a specific tree for you and describe it to me. It does not matter if you do not know the name of it: it is only important that you see it clearly in your mind's eye. Take your time in selecting it and remember that it may change later if a different tree is more appropriate for you. When your tree has appeared, look at it carefully so that its form will be imprinted on your memory and you can bring it back at will. Now, actually imagine that you are walking over to it and putting your arms around the trunk, feeling the energy in it. Pull away from time to time, but with your arms still around it to test its strength and solidity. Now turn around and lean your spine against the trunk, either standing or sitting on the ground, whichever you prefer. Feel the firm trunk against your back and consciously lean all your weight against it, allowing it to support you entirely. Let yourself feel the joy and relief of having the tree support you so completely and relax. Tell yourself that this reliance is a healthy one, for it will strengthen rather than weaken you as leaning on another human being can do. Now try to tune into the tree, identifying with it as much as you can, trying to become one with it. You will now begin to feel how the roots reach thirstily, deep down into the earth, to draw up the food the tree needs to help it to flourish and grow tall and strong. Try to feel as if you too are drawing up from the depths of the earth just what you most need to nourish and sustain you from the Earth Mother. With each indrawn breath, consciously draw this vital good up into you, to flow throughout your whole system. With each outgoing breath, let go of any fears, doubts, anxieties, or other negative emotions which could block the benefit you are receiving from this influx of energy. Repeat this slowly, concentrating on the breath and allowing yourself to experience the comfort and satisfaction you will begin to feel.

Now, consciously select certain attributes, such as love, compassion, tenderness, reassurance, which you have craved from your own mother and which she, being human, could not always give you, however much she may have tried. Drink all you need from the fount and let go of anything which is blocking the flow.

When you have had your fill, turn your attention up to the leaves and branches of your tree, reaching up towards the sky to draw down from the sun's rays the energy and light from the Solar Father which, together with the food from the Earth Mother, will strengthen and help every part of you to grow as it does for the tree. Again, with each inhalation fill yourself with this solar energy and, with each exhalation, let go of anything which could impede this process, such as fear and doubt or unworthiness.

As you continue to breathe deeply, allow to enter your mind all the attributes of a father which you have missed as a child in your own father, such as courage, wisdom, understanding, and acceptance. Allow yourself to take your fill of these and let them flow into the empty spaces within you.

Spend a short time suspended between both Parents, inhaling their joint attributes and exhaling any blocks to this new-found source of nourishment. Now slowly turn and face the tree and thank it for all it has given you, and quietly move back into full consciousness, bringing with you all you have experienced and promising to return regularly to the tree to be renewed.

If you have access to any actual tree, you can go through the whole exercise while physically leaning against its trunk, looking down into the earth and then up into the sky as you proceed. This very often helps to give a sense of reality to the exercise, especially at the beginning when it may seem rather strange.

This exercise should be practised at least once every day, but there is no limit and you may wish to go through it several times, especially if you are feeling weak or insecure for any reason."

## Connecting to Cosmic Parents

The next step is to have the person invoke his own version of the Cosmic Parents in order to bring him into contact with them in a deeper and more personal way. This is especially helpful for those who have had very negative parents, or who have lost one or both during childhood and suffer from a deep inner hunger for love and acceptance. In most cases, it is better to connect a person to one Cosmic Parent at a time, asking the High C to indicate which one should be contacted first.

We begin by repeating the tree exercise, with which the person will already be familiar from his daily practice. After directing him to take a few breaths to make the connection with each of the Cosmic Parents, we suggest that he ask one of them to appear as a person so that it will be easier for him to make a deeper and more intimate contact. We explain that they usually appear as figures, but occasionally as symbols and that he should describe what he sees on his inner screen.

If a person is unable to visualize a figure as a personification of the Cosmic Parent, it is invariably because he has no clear idea of what a positive parent should be. He may see a symbol instead, which is a clear indication that he is not yet able to make a more personal contact. In such cases, we suggest that he visualize this symbol each day until he is accustomed to the new experience of being nourished by it on a deep level of his being, at which time he can return and seek contact with a more personal aspect of the Cosmic Parents. If he reports that a figure appears, we ask which of the Cosmic Parents has come to replace his human one.

If the Cosmic Mother has come first, we direct him to wait until the picture becomes very clear and he feels that she is right there with him. Sometimes a person will take off from here as if it were exactly what he had been waiting for without realizing it. In this way many deep and very poignant experiences have resulted, accompanied by floods of tears, or expressions of joy. However, not everyone is free enough to proceed on his own, in which case we direct him in whatever way is indicated by the High C.

If the Cosmic Mother has personified, we might say: 'Perhaps you would like to imagine yourself as a little child again and climb up into her ample lap, feel her arms around you, her hand caressing your head as you press your face against her body. Maybe you would like to suckle at her breast, or do anything else which comes to your mind which will satisfy your deepest needs." As he becomes more and more involved in the inner scene, we encourage him to express whatever emotions rise to the surface, such as relief or sorrow for past loneliness. Many people take advantage of this opportunity to express all the hurts, disappointments, feelings of rejection and lack of acceptance, and many old repressed memories as they surface, together with the emotions which have been buried with them. We always suggest that the person express these feelings as freely as possible, either silently or aloud, whichever way helps him to accept whatever he needs from the new parent. Naturally, the deeper the emotions the more therapeutic the experience will be; but not everyone is ready to handle strong emotions so the guide for the session must be sure to stay tuned into the High C for directions. This is particularly necessary when the person is expressing very negative emotions, as it is imperative to know how long it is advisable to let him stay with each one. Then the guide can suggest a ritual bath or that the person erase the whole scene as if from a blackboard.

Often a person will go back to specific incidents in childhood of his own accord, and so helpful has this proved to be that we make a point of suggesting that he ask to be taken back to any incident which needs to be healed. Perhaps he craved love, understanding and acceptance, and instead was ignored, laughed at or rejected. If the mother was the cause of his distress, we ask if he would like to take his newly-found Cosmic Mother back into the unhappy experience and see how she would have acted under similar circumstances, since she is capable of giving him exactly what he needed but did not receive from his human mother. In this way many old traumas are released and healed, and the sense of freedom following such a catharsis is often tremendous.

If the Cosmic Father appears, the procedure is similar except that with a male figure the experiences are, of course, different. We first suggest that the person ask for a personification of the Cosmic Father to appear and, if he is free enough to take it on his own from there, we merely ask questions from time to time to keep the experience flowing. It is interesting that the most frequent need is to be taken seriously and accepted by the father figure, and having it met by the Cosmic Father is often sufficient to satisfy the person making the contact.

If the natural father was weak, it is advisable to suggest that the person approach his new Cosmic Father as a child and feel the strength and the security of the father's arms and the comfort of being filled with strength and courage. As with the Cosmic Mother, it is often advisable to have the person take him back into specific incidents in childhood and watch as he behaves very differently from the human father by bringing support and wisdom to each situation instead of rejection and criticism. All kinds of pent-up emotions, resentments, anger, frustration and misunderstandings come tumbling out, often accompanied by tears, groans, swearing, and at times even screams as these emotions are released.

It is very important to assure each person that the one guiding him through this inner journey is not acting in the role of a judge, but is present merely to help him to let go as completely as possible anything from the past which could be holding him back from growth towards wholeness.

One warning: in order to lead another human being through such an experience, the guide *must* be tuned into the High C, as only in that way can he be sure of knowing how far to let the experience go and when to end the session. One young man was so neglected by both of his parents that he could take only a very few minutes of contact with each of the Cosmic Parents who appeared to him. He reminded me of the stories about some of the inmates of concentration camps who, when released, could eat only very small amounts of food at a time and if given more would vomit. Fortunately, this young man was acutely aware of his starved condition and knew that he could take only very short visits with his new loving parents. Each person's needs are so individual and there is no simple formula, so it is essential for both partners to stay tuned in to the High C for direction, which is the only really safe way to do this work.

## Symbols for the High C

At a certain stage in the work it becomes desirable for a person to find a specific symbol or figure to represent the High C. Since people are in human form, it is much easier for them to communicate with a similar form. The Teaching Forces which have guided us through the years have indicated that they are indeed forces, not personalities, and that for our benefit they often personify to make it easier for us to receive their teaching. We have always referred to them as specialists', as they seem to assume different forms to fit specific problems.

There are many different symbols for the High C, the most common ones from the West being Christ and the Virgin Mary; from the Orient, Buddha and Quan Yin; and from India, any of the many aspects of God such as Krishna, Shiva, Vishnu, Ganesh. In addition there are many other numinous figures depending upon which aspect of the God Force is to be contacted at the time includ-ing *gurus* and saints.

Since I am a devotee of Sri Sathya Sai Baba, his image is the one which for me symbolizes the God within, or High C, and he frequently appears in the waking dream sessions in that capacity, advising, teaching and healing, wherever such are needed.

So when the time is right for a person to make a more conscious contact with his own High C, preferably after he has released from the human forms in which he had hoped to find his security, we suggest that he call on the High C to reveal itself to him. To initiate this contact, we erect the triangle as usual, and then using his side of the triangle like a telephone wire, we suggest that he call on his own High Self to appear to him in visible form. However, it does not always appear in human form. Sometimes a symbol will enter his mind such as the sun or a hand or a light. One young girl timidly explained that she was seeing an anchor and asked if that would be okay. Actually, it could not have been more perfect for her as she was one of those people who seemed to float ten feet above the ground most of the time, her feet rarely touching the earth and therefore out of touch with reality as we know it. She decided to hang the anchor around her neck to help to ground her.

When the symbol or figure is clear, it is most helpful if the person asks it to accompany him back into childhood, and help him to recall any particularly painful or frightening episodes, and to give him support and a sense of protection while facing them. The presence of this positive authority figure is an extraordinary help in re-evaluating old negative experiences, in receiving healing of deep hurts or sorrows, and in draining off energy which has been locked away in painful memories and therefore unavailable for use in everyday life. We often suggest that the person engage in conversation with this figure and, in this way, many answers to all kinds of problems are revealed.

The symbol or figure representing the High C does not necessarily remain the same each time it appears as it seems to take whatever form is the most appropriate for the occasion and for the particular problem for which help is being sought. For example, one young man saw the Christ figure, but His robe was of the blue usually worn by the Virgin Mary in paintings. It turned out that his need that day was for the Mother aspect to appear to him to bring the love and comfort he was not given by his own mother.

Once a figure has appeared, the person knows without doubt that it is always within reach but that he must call on it for help. The figure of the High C is an enormous source of comfort and strength for those who have been able to make contact with it. They report that they never again feel so lonely or bereft, for they know help is close at hand if they seek it.

Chapter 8

# THE INNER CHILD

During the continuing process of self-discovery, after the separation from the parents, an Inner Child often comes into view either in the sessions or in a dream. This child needs attention and often healing and we have been shown many different ways to do this. The child needs to be helped to grow into maturity so that it can be absorbed into the central core of the person, together with all the other facets of the personality which have come to light from within.

This child can be male or female depending on which aspect of the person has remained immature, and it can be of any age, depending on when in the person's life, the event or situation occurred which caused the Inner Child to remain at that level instead of growing up with the person's other aspects.

As soon as the Inner Child has surfaced from the unconscious, where it had been hidden from sight, it is essential for the person to be led back in memory so that he can face the old painful situation, but from an adult point of view. Often an authority figure, such as a personification of the High C, is needed to accompany him. This supportive figure is especially helpful if the incident was a severely traumatic one, or if a great deal of fear is present at the thought of reviewing it, as this figure can be called upon to heal, comfort and give him the needed support.

Some of the most traumatic incidents we encounter are beatings and rejection by one or both parents; perhaps the most damaging of all are sexual abuse and incest, which we have come to realize are much more common than is generally suspected. Both affect the victim's life in many negative ways, the most damaging of which is the effect on his sexual life and his choice of a mate. Two examples among many come to my mind, each one different but equally disruptive.

One young girl who was engaged to be married but filled with fear at the prospect of the sexual activity involved in marriage, asked if I could help her to discover the reason for this deep-seated fear. As soon as she was relaxed, we both asked that she be led by her High C back to any incident in her early life which she had repressed, and which might have caused this fear which outweighed her very real love for the man she was planning to marry. She looked back slowly over the years and suddenly an incident flashed into her mind which occurred when she was about eight years of age. She recounted that some older boys bullied her into going with them behind a high wall behind the school which they all attended. As soon as they were out of sight, they started to pull down her panties and molested her despite her struggles and cries for help. After it was all over, they left her terrified and bruised. She ran home to tell her parents what had happened, hysterically crying as she did so. Her father was furious and threatened to report the boys. But they only laughed and spread the rumour around the small town where they all lived that it was she who had enticed them to participate in sexual activities as she was that kind of a girl. Her family was poor and lived on the wrong side of the tracks, while the boys were all from wealthy and prominent families and their word was believed in preference to that of the girl. She was branded as loose and rejected by many of her friends whose mothers forbade them to associate with her. Thus she suffered rejection, yet had been innocent of any of the things of which she was accused.

The man who wished to marry her was the son of a prominent family. They had met while attending the same college. She had worked hard to rise above her lowly state by educating herself with the help of a scholarship. The two young people were well-suited to one another, having many interests in common and there was every indication that the marriage would be successful if she could free herself from her dread of sex.

When she was able, while in the reverie, to look at the incident, from her present adult point of view, she could see how, as a little girl, she had been the victim of forces beyond her ability to control. She realized that there was no valid reason for the terrible guilt which she had carried with her all through the years, or for the shame caused by the jeers of her peer group who had been told lies instead of the true facts. She also saw that she had risen above her humble birth and had made a place for herself in the world as a competent woman and that she must not allow this old suppressed memory to haunt her any longer and prevent her from accepting what life was now offering her: a fine husband and the promise of a happy future.

I told her to imagine that she was taking the little eight year old girl to a river in which she could bathe her and wash off all the old feelings of being unworthy and besmirched, which she did thankfully. She then took the child in her arms, dried her and dressed her in a fresh clean dress, combed her hair and soothed her, and talked to her as if she were her own little daughter. I suggested that she imagine taking the little girl back inside herself so that this part of her could grow up and unite with all the other parts of herself, and that she should take her out for a few minutes every day in order to continue the communication between them and to give the child part of herself the assurance of being loved and accepted. Then I asked her to visualize a path which would lead to a beautiful green meadow filled with flowers where she could take off her shoes and run and dance as carefree as a child, to express joy at her new freedom. When she had finally let herself go and had danced away all her old fears, I told her to imagine that her *fiancé* was approaching her and that she could run to meet him and tell him the good news of her new-found freedom. She was able to do this easily, to my surprise as much as to her's, since she had been terrified when she started this inner journey.

She was able to continue visualizing the scene and when she came to the embrace and could feel his arms around her, I left the room for a few minutes while she imagined the two of them coming together in an embrace of love on all levels like a dress rehearsal before the actual experience. When I returned to the room, I could tell from her face that she had lost her former fears.

She and *her fiancé* were married and in time became the proud parents of a fine healthy son. Fortunately, her husband was an unusually gentle, patient and understanding man who helped her to act out her release from her old fears and guilt.

The other case which comes to mind is that of a young woman whose problem was that she compulsively prostituted herself by having intercourse with most unsuitable partners, none of whom she liked, let alone loved. She hated herself for these escapades and desperately wanted to stop this way of life, as she felt soiled after each episode. Again, we could find nothing in her conscious memory to account for this behaviour except that she had always had a very poor self-image. Despite the fact that she was always striving to improve herself in every way, the feeling of worthlessness still haunted her and became even stronger after each sexual experience. She was really desperate. This is often the best state to be in when seeking help as many people seem to have to hurt very badly before they are willing to start the hard and painful work to change themselves.

It took longer than usual to relax her, as she was tense due to her desperate anxiety about finding the cause of her problem. We erected the triangle and asked to be shown whatever she needed to know, experience, or see, which would help to release her from her self-hatred. I then suggested that she visualize a road ahead of her and start walking along it, observing all that appeared along the way as she looked to see where it was taking her. After a short while she gasped and said that she could see a house which she recognized as one in which she had lived as a child, but which she had completely forgotten although she remembered seeing a picture of it in an old family album and had asked at the time whose house it was. I encouraged her to approach it and to enter by the front door as if she were herself invisible but could observe everything or anyone in the house. She was extremely hesitant which clued me into the possibility that we were close to discovering something which had happened in this house to cause her problem, and that we might not have to search for the key further back in time. So, with many questions, such as "Do you see anyone in the house?", I gently but firmly encouraged her to tell me anything she could see whether it seemed to be important or not, explaining that seemingly small and insignificant incidents often cause serious problems if they are blown up in size and importance in the child's mind at the time.

This reassurance seemed to relax her and she began to describe some of the objects she could see in the various rooms. After a while she was very quiet for longer than usual. I was prompted from the High C not to break the silence, but to send a request to her High C to help her to uncover whatever it was that was buried here. Suddenly, a wracking sob escaped from her throat and she cried out, "No! No! Not that!"

I assured her that it was of the utmost importance for her to be freed from whatever it was that she was seeing which was causing such acute distress and that I was present not as a judge but only to help her. Finally, through her sobs, she managed to blurt out what she had seen and, piece by piece, was able to describe how her father had molested her sexually when she was so young that she did not fully understand what it was all about.

At the same time she was terrified by his threats of the terrible consequences if she ever told anyone about their relationship which made her realize, young though she was, that there was something wrong about it. She was able to recall how her father had always referred to her as a bad girl, which she realized was to cover up his own guilt. Apparently the mother knew about the relationship but was so afraid of her husband, who was a violent man, that it was easier to close her eyes to it instead of dealing with it. She too called her daughter a bad girl, but with venom, as she was jealous of her husband's attentions to her daughter and his neglect of herself. This poor child had no support or love from either of her parents so it is no wonder that she felt so unworthy. She sought love anywhere she could find it, but preferably in the most degrading and painful situations possible since this was the original pattern for her sexual activities. She felt she was worthless and, because her parents had programmed her to feel this way about herself, she felt she rated only a negative type of experience.

She also suffered from guilt as a result of the incestuous relationship with her father which she had later understood but completely repressed. She punished herself by degrading herself in every way possible to pay for her early wrongdoing.

As soon as she became quieter, I suggested that she look at that little girl who was still very much alive within her but still stuck at that early age and still suffering from those old feelings of guilt and shame. I asked her if she would like to take her in her arms and reassure her, and give her that love she so craved. This brought a fresh gush of sobs as she cried, "Yes, yes, more than anything in the world I would like to do that." She literally threw herself into visualizing bathing the child, combing her hair, rubbing healing oil all over her and caressing and fondling her as if she were her own beloved child.

I then told her to sing to the child to lull her to sleep, which she immediately started to do. She obviously could not do enough for the child now that she was being given the opportunity to take responsibility for her. As soon as she reported that the child was fast asleep, I asked if she would like to talk to her while she slept and give suggestions that the ugly past events were merely a dream or nightmare and that when she awoke every part would be forgotten. She eagerly followed this suggestion and spoke to the child exactly as if she were of flesh and blood. Then I suggested that she call on her own High C and ask it to reveal itself in the form of a symbol or person that would heal the child as she lay asleep.

She was not at all sure that she could do this but said she would try and, to her surprise, there came into her inner scene the figure of Christ. As is often the case, he was wearing a robe the colour of Mother Mary's, a wonderful deep blue. I asked her to inquire about the reason for this and she replied in an awestruck voice, "Oh, it is the Father robed as the Mother, so it is both of them in one." With that insight, she literally collapsed in tears, this time not from pain, but from joy and utter relief for she had found a new mother and father combined within herself.

She then told me that she still felt unclean and therefore hesitant to allow this figure to touch her, so I asked if she would like to bathe herself as she had bathed the little girl. She replied instantly, "Yes, in the sea", and went on to explain that the salt water would cleanse her. I told her to take off all her clothes and to put them in a pile and set fire to them as they must be replaced by new ones since they represented old attitudes. She did so with real abandon and described how she stamped out the fire and then buried the ashes deep in the earth as she wanted every trace of them gone forever. She was then free to run into the sea and splash around in the salt water, making sure to wash all over her body so that every trace of the old blemishes was. removed. I then suggested that she choose a way to express her new-found freedom and she immediately told me that she would like to be a dolphin and glide freely in the sea from the sheer joy of being alive.

When she finally told me she had come out of the water, I handed her a white dress, symbolizing purity, which she gladly took and put on almost reverently. I then told her to go forth into life again with the secret knowledge that she was cleansed of all her past experiences and of the guilt and self-loathing which had resulted from them, and that she now had a new self-image.

Shortly after this session she met a fine man who had lost his wife in a car accident and was left with two young children. Their relationship was a little frightening for her at first, as she had no pattern for a close loving relationship with a man, so she came back asking for help and another reverie to show her what she needed to know to be able to take on this challenge.

I took her in imagination back to the beach where she had bathed in the sea in the last session and suggested that she lie on the sand in the sun and relax as if she were lying on a real beach. When she seemed quite relaxed, I told her to give the direction to her body to remain relaxed while she visualized the man who had asked her to marry him walking slowly along the beach looking for her. At first she tensed, but when she saw that he too was apprehensive about a new relationship, she forgot her own fears and waved to him to join her. When she told me that he was lying beside her on the sand I directed her to allow the scene to unfold without repressing it and to ask the High C to help them both to overcome their fears together. I left the room for a few minutes to give her more freedom to relax into the inner experience and when I returned I found her radiant. She told me that she had lost her old fear and felt satisfied that she could be a good wife to this man and a good mother to his children.

Her *fiancé* asked to see me a few days later. He told me that he was still sad over his first wife's death and felt that he needed to cut the ties which connected them before embarking on a new marriage. I explained the preliminary Figure Eight exercise, which he agreed to practise daily for the next two weeks.

At the end of that time he arrived to cut the ties to his wife. When he was about to describe to me where the ties were attached each of them he suddenly stopped in the middle of a sentence. I asked him what had happened and he told me in a strained voice that he had the distinct impression that his wife, whom he could see clearly, was just as anxious as he was to have the ties connecting them severed. I explained that he could talk to her, ask question and receive her answers in the form of thoughts. He replied that this must be what was happening and that she seemed to be telling him that she hoped that he would remarry, and that she would give him and his new wife her blessing as she would be so thankful that her children would again have a mother's care.

He wept as he recounted what his wife was telling him and told me that it had never occurred to him that he would be able to have such a convincing and real experience. He was obviously deeply moved but at the same time completely amazed at what was happening on the inner scene.

We proceeded with the remaining part of the session and he described how he detached the ties which connected him to his wife and how he embraced her and gave her his blessing as he watched her move off into a different dimension of consciousness appearing to be radiantly happy to be free to leave the world she had known as his wife.

The new marriage took place shortly after and the girl who had been rejected and besmirched as a child found happiness with her husband and was able to love his children as she had learned to love her own Inner Child. They both look forward to the birth of their own baby with joy.

These are just two examples out of hundreds. Each person has a different child part of himself locked deep within which needs to be released, healed and cared for so that it can mature and become a consciously functioning part of the whole person. This release unlocks the energy stored away with the old memories so that it can be used in daily life.

There are, of course, many other stories less dramatic than these two but in every case the person is urged to take responsibility for the child within and bring it out daily for personal attention until it appears fully grown and can be absorbed into the main personality.

## Rejection

Any act of rejection, whether conscious or unconscious on the part of the person responsible for it, is apt to affect the behaviour of the one rejected in a negative fashion. We have all heard of cases of parents who have such a strong desire for a child of a particular sex that one or both are violently emotional in their expressions of disappointment if the child is not of the sex they wanted. Such a reaction by the parents is registered by the baby as rejection which has a lifelong effect, because the baby's entry into this world was linked to insecurity and non-acceptance by the two people who should be its prime security. Such early rejection, even in cases where both parents are eventually able to love the child, sets the stage for a wide variety of negative reactions to life. Some people will actually seek situations where they will be rejected, as rejection is a familiar condition and, therefore, in a strange way secure to them. Other people go through life always demanding love and attention to assuage their hunger for acceptance but are never satisfied, no matter how much they receive.

Other reasons besides the unwanted sex of a child can cause parents to turn away from a baby at birth or in its early years. Some parents are upset if the baby is not attractive at birth, or does not develop as fast as other babies of the same age, particularly those belonging to friends or relatives, amongst whom competition can be fierce. Whatever the cause, rejection results in a great deal of future pain and misery; if the rejection is uncovered and the pain released, the person can be shown a true picture of himself without the overlay of disappointment projected onto him by the parents, which causes him to feel that he will never be able to satisfy them.

When we are asked to help someone suffering from an unusually strong fear of rejection, we first try to uncover the cause. This often comes to light when we take him through the puberty rites or when he is going through the lists of his parents' attributes. Just knowing the cause of his problem in some cases, is sufficient to free the person from its effect. However, a complete forgiveness of the parent or other rejecting person is always necessary before true freedom can be experienced.

Sometimes the rejection felt by a child was unavoidable, as in the case of the loss of one or both parents at an early age, before the conscious mind had developed sufficiently for the loss to be explained and understood in its true light as being beyond the power of the parent to prevent. As it was still interpreted by the child as rejection, it must be faced and dealt with in order for the adult to be free of its effects and to begin consciously to acquire different attitudes.

Two such situations illustrate this point. One involves a young man who never knew his mother, who died shortly after his birth. He was brought up by his maternal grandparents who never lost an opportunity to tell him that he was the cause of their dear daughter's death. This added a sense of guilt to his original feeling of rejection by his mother.

I guided him as an adult spectator back to the time of his mother's death and urged him to talk to his mother and ask her to explain to him how she felt when she realized that she was about to leave her newborn infant. He related to me that she was telling him how anxious and sad she felt and how worried she was at the thought of him being left without her love and attention so soon after he was freed from her womb in which he had been so secure and safe. He began to cry quietly as this strange conversation proceeded and he was able to see the difference between what he had felt was rejection and the reluctant parting which she was describing to him on this inner level. He sobbed when she assured him that it was not his fault that she had died.

I asked him if he would like to ask her forgiveness for his mistake in feeling that she had rejected him. He gladly accepted the opportunity, so I guided him through the part of the puberty rite involving forgiving the parent and asking her for forgiveness. As he went through this ritual it was as if a heavy load fell away from him and he was able to tell his mother how sorry he was for the years of misunderstanding on his part.

Another example involving rejection was that of a young woman whose father died when she was between two and three years of age. She could clearly remember sitting on his lap while he read his newspaper; being picked up and hugged when he came home each evening, and many more such loving little actions which she had become used to expecting from him. After his death, she desperately missed his affection and, as she grew older, she pushed her sadness deep down inside of her where she thought it would not hurt her so much.

During the routine session of cutting the ties to her father, everything she had repressed came tumbling out in anger and resentment that he had left her all alone and had gone away. She was shocked and horrified at her own outburst as she had had no idea of the deep feelings of anger she had pressed down and out of sight.

I told her to allow herself to be that little girl again, which she was easily able to do. She told me she could see herself as a child of about two years of age. I then suggested that she pretend that she was eagerly waiting for her father to come home at the end of the day and to tell me all that had happened and how she felt. She described how she could hear his key in the lock of the door and how she ran to meet him, and how he called her by a pet name, asked if she had had a happy day, and picked her up in his arms and hugged and kissed her, calling her his little princess. As she described the scene, I could tell that she was really back there in her memory. She described how she could feel his strong arms around her and his hand stroking her hair and many other little intimate acts.

I told her to pour out her heart to him, to tell him how desperately she missed him, and to ask him to tell her why he had left her. She was able to do this easily and finally asked him to forgive her for harbouring anger and resentment against him all these years. She could also forgive him for his seeming desertion of her now that she was able to *feel* the understanding which before she had only known intellectually. She understood that he had had no choice and had grieved at having to leave her as much as she had suffered at his loss. At this point I suggested that she now take the little girl in her arms as if she were her own child and love and console her as her father had once done. I urged her to do this every day and to imagine the child with her all the time.

She came out of this session more relaxed than I had ever seen her, and she said she felt as if a heavy load had dropped away from her. She continued to work consciously to change her old pattern of expecting rejection from men and slowly achieved a more positive self-image to replace the one of the rejected little girl for whom she now chose to take responsibility.

Sometimes the act of rejection appears on the surface to be too slight to cause a future problem, but we have discovered that it is the way in which a child reacts to a situation rather than the seriousness of the act of rejection which determines the effect. An illustration of this point involves a woman who had often been allowed to take a shower with her father as a little girl and had eagerly anticipated this closeness with him each time. Inevitably, one day, out of childish curiosity, she reached up to touch his penis and was startled at his violent reaction. He removed her not only from the shower but from the bathroom and locked the door, and from that day she was never again allowed to join him in the shower. No explanation was given for this abrupt banishment so she never understood the reason for it and, being too young to make the obvious connection between her innocent act and the immediate rejection, she was left with a deep hurt and an unsolved mystery.

The result of her reaction to this incident was that, despite her very loving nature, she was never able to participate in an intimate relationship with a man, a situation which she had been completely unable to understand or alleviate until she finally uncovered the root cause. It is still too soon to know the result of her discovery, but she is now confident that she will be able to act more freely and hopes eventually to lose this old pattern now that she is aware of its cause.

# Chapter 9

# ANIMUS AND ANIMA
# MALE AND FEMALE ASPECTS
# WITHIN WOMEN AND MEN

There is another very important reason for evaluating the effect of the parents on a person: in many cases they have influenced his choice of a mate. Carl Jung presented to the world his theory that within every man lies a female aspect which he called anima and, likewise, in every woman there is a male aspect, which he called animus.

The patterns for the male and female aspects in a person are laid down as they react to the examples of masculinity and feminity illustrated by their parents. Because these patterns develop unconsciously, they are not aware of the process and think they are always acting as a free individual when choosing a mate.

The ideal relationship between the two sides of a male should be that the male part is dominant with the feminine aspect supporting and co-operating with it. For a woman, the feminine part should be stronger with the masculine helping in the background. The balance can be upset in any number of different ways according to how a person reacted to his parents' attitudes to their own sex. In addition, a person is born with certain tendencies which were inherited or even brought over from a past life.

We have all seen extreme cases of men who are all male, have little contact with their anima, and who therefore lack the ability to feel; and we have seen women who are totally feminine but who are out of touch with their animus and lack the ability to think clearly.

There are two other extremes or caricatures as we sometimes call such clearly defined cases: men who have such a strong anima that they appear effeminate and women whose animus controls them to such an extent that they become dominating and forceful and act more like men.

We have been shown many ways to help correct such imbalances. The first step is to scrutinize the parents' attitudes and to try to understand their effect on the developing child. A chain reaction is often involved, the parents having been exposed to their parents' patterns and so on back through past generations, each one repeating the habits of the preceeding one. One reason for this repetition is that a man is likely to be attracted to a mate who reminds him of his mother if he has had a good relationship with her, or to a woman who is very different from her if he reacted to her with rebellion or dislike. The same rule applies when a woman chooses a husband or lover. She will usually be attracted to a man who reminds her of her father, or who is as different as possible from him if she disliked him. Unfortunately, people then project onto a mate all of the attributes they have become accustomed to associating with their ideal. The poor person who is expected to carry these projections is then invariably forced to live out a role which has been held up as an example instead of being free to express his real self. After the parental ties have been cut and the lists of the positive and negative attributes of the parents have been compiled, it is important for each person to study these in order to see how his parents have affected him.

One young man with whom I had been working on the release from his mother called me and very excitedly told me about an insight which had just occurred to him. He realized that he was emotionally very like his mother and, therefore, guilty of some of the very attitudes he criticized in her. He said that he also realized that one of the chief causes of his divorce from his wife was that she had tried to point out to him these same similarities between him and his mother, but before he was ready to see them or knew how to deal with them. People can only see and accept such aspects of themselves when they are ready to work on them and are offered a method for doing so.

We have also observed that in the majority of cases a person has to be really suffering for some reason before he is forced by his pain or discomfort to make a decision to seek help. Most people are apt to be lazy when life is running smoothly and they are not forced in any way to change. Many people tend to resist change, preferring whatever is known and secure, however unsatisfactory it may be, to the unknown and often frightening alternative.

The suffering which can push them to take control of reshaping themselves can have a financial, emotional, physical or mental cause. Whatever situation a person is faced with that he cannot handle on his own can force him to seek help to find a way to solve the problem causing his suffering. The painful experience can then be a blessing in disguise, leading him to freedom.

It is a big task for a person to start to reshape himself and the task can loom like a huge mountain before him, making him feel utterly inadequate to climb to the top. He needs to be reminded that it does not have to be scaled in one leap, but must be taken a step at a time. As with any task, it is too overpowering to attack it as a whole, but anyone can begin to work on one small part at a time and, before long, will have made more progress than he ever dreamed would be possible, as each small piece is joined to others, like pieces in a jigsaw puzzle.

## Sirens and Medusa-like Women

There are certain men who come under the spell of so-called 'Medusa women'. These men are invariably very successful in their careers, which makes it all the more surprising that they should be so taken over by such women.

Like the sirens of the old myths and fairy tales, who lured men to their death with the aid of their feminine wiles and protestations of love, these modern versions do the same. It is as if they throw a magic philtre into the man's eyes to blind him to reality and thus keep him under their spell. They are themselves overshadowed by the Medusa archetype, which renders them inhumanly powerful, and they can paralyze their prey and turn the poor men to stone, as a single snake can paralyze a rabbit or other small animal.

These are not the castrating animus-controlled women. They are all feminine but lack the balance of the animus and so they need to find the masculine image outside of themselves. This is why they project their animus onto very masculine men who lack a strong anima and who, in turn, are seeking their anima outside of themselves in such a woman. The two people are locked into a tight embrace by their mutual need, each as helpless as the other to break the spell that binds them together in a monstrous embrace.

These women appear to the men they attract as sweet, loving and worshipful, but at the same time they are destroying them as the black widow spider kills her mate when she has coupled with him. The men in the grip of such women enjoy the relationship in a perverse way, misinterpreting it for love, and feeling, in a strange way fulfilled and completed.

These women, who appear to be so feminine, are actually the aggressors and play with the man like a cat with a mouse, sometimes even leaving him, only to return again and again to lure him back even more strongly into their power. They do not always marry the man, preferring to steal him from another woman. Frequently in such a situation it is the wife who seeks help to free her husband from the clutches of such a woman. It is not enough to free him from her. He must be filled with a positive force and helped to understand what happened so that he can avoid pulling in again the same woman or another of the same type. In addition, it is advisable for the man to be helped to develop his own inner woman or feeling function, so that he will not be overpowered by such human sirens again.

When working with a woman overshadowed by the Medusa archetype, it is necessary to call on a positive archetypal figure to help with both the man's release as well as her own.

**Homosexuality**

We have been shown that homosexuality stems from several different causes. The concept of reincarnation offers a possible explanation for homosexuality. According to this concept a person reincarnates not only into different cultures and periods, but as both men and women, during his many lives. So it seems likely that confusion can occur when a changeover from a life as a member of one sex to that of the other is taking place. The reincarnating soul brings with it many of the former characteristics from past personalities and, when these are very strong, they can easily overshadow the new personality. Thus, a strong man reincarnating in a female body in a new life might easily continue to behave like a man. Likewise, a very feminine woman, reborn into a male body, would find it hard to be an aggressive male. The sex change seems to be further complicated if. in the former life, the person had been very active sexually and strongly attached to sexual gratification.

People acquire their patterns for feminity and masculinity from their parents by either copying them or rebelling against them. This affects their psyche and their animus or anima, the man's psyche being influenced by his father and his anima by his mother, and a woman's psyche by her mother and animus by her father. In addition, they unconsciously react to the parents' attitudes, not only to their own sex but also to that of their mate.

The chain reaction of children responding to their parents who responded to their own parents can be broken when people begin to work on the balance of masculine and feminine within themselves and understand the concepts of animus and anima.

**Marriage or Bonding**

I was once shown in a reverie that the closest relationships, such as between members of a family, were the ones which could teach us the most. This definitely applies to marriage partners. However, if both members are willing to work on themselves, it is an invaluable help if they will both visualize the triangle uniting them at the High C. If they will then ask for help and direction from the High C instead of trying to work out their problems themselves with only their conscious minds, the partnership will be far more rewarding as well as mutually helpful to each person.

Also, if instead of relying on one another's strong points, they will strengthen their own weak areas, they will have a chance to break the symbiotic relationship, which so often develops between two people. In some cases, the two partners are locked together like a pair of octopuses and it is not unusual for one or both of them to resist breaking this double clasp. Preferring to continue to lean on one another, a condition which has become familiar and therefore provides a false security. This is especially true when the relationship is of long duration and strong habits have been established. In such cases, the death of one of the partners can be a devastating shock to the one left alone; a man or woman can fall apart after the death of a spouse and be unable to stand on their own feet when the human leaning post has been removed.

The ideal, of course, is for two people who love one another to be willing to help each other to bring about a better balance in each. This involves toning down the over-developed functions or qualities and strengthening the weak ones, so that both can stand erect, neither using the other as a leaning post. When this mutual help is put into practice, a healthy, flowing and more alive partnership can begin to develop, with both partners helping one another towards wholeness rather than interdependence. If this is accomplished before the death of one of them, the separation will be a great deal easier. The one left behind will also be able to make a better adjustment to the change of life style and the inevitable loneliness which results from the loss of the partner. However, not everyone is willing to initiate any kind of change and many will, in fact, fight it.

I am reminded of one young man who stormed at me for endangering his marriage by teaching his wife the Figure Eight exercise. In vain, I tried to break through the tirade to try to explain that, far from breaking the marriage, this exercise could greatly improve it by allowing each person his or her own space within it. But he had his wife so completely under his domination that she hardly dared to take a breath without first asking his permission. She herself had reached a crisis and knew that to survive as an individual she must, at all cost, put a halt to her servitude. Unfortunately, in this particular case, the marriage did end in divorce, but this was not the fault of the Figure Eight. It was entirely due to the inflexibility of the husband's will and his insistence on attempting to reduce his wife to the position of a slave with no rights of her own. In his eyes she had been born for one purpose: to cater to his every whim. The wife had to be really desperate to make the decision to change the situation, as is often the case before the necessary courage can be mustered to take a stand. One hopes that this woman will not undertake a new relationship until she has worked further on herself or she will attract a similar man with whom she will repeat the old negative pattern. The husband, on the other hand, may have to repeat the pattern, and have each marriage end in divorce before he realizes that he himself is responsible for the failures.

The triangle can also be used most successfully in relation to sex. If both the man and woman will seek union with each other at the High C rather than across the base of the triangle at the personality or physical level only, the experience will be raised to a very high vibration of mutual fulfillment which far surpasses the usual one of mutual gratification. Both participants will be filled with a flow of energy from their High Self, instead of just from the personality level.

Chapter 10

# CUTTING TIES TO OTHER RELATIONSHIPS

Those children whose parents realize the wisdom of releasing their hold on them when they reach the age of puberty are very fortunate indeed. Naturally, parents must be the authority figures until the child is ready to start developing his own independence from them and begins to stand on his own two feet in the world of men and women. Some parents with whom we have worked are really anxious to release their ties to their children. However, this should never be attempted before the age of puberty, which varies from person to person. The ritual is similar to the one already described for the separation by the grown child from his parents.

In the case where an adolescent is to be released by his parents, I usually suggest that each parent end the ritual by placing him in the care of his own High C. This is done by suggesting that the parent visualize a triangle between himself and his child with a line of light flowing down from the High C and into the child's head. We have been told that this is the most effective exercise anyone can do for a close family member, though a broken line should be visualized if the 'child' is an adult, so that he is free to make the line solid and to make contact with his High C when he is ready to do so.

It is also important for parents to cut the ties to any children who have died, whatever their age at death, to ensure their easy release after death and to lessen the duration of the parents' mourning. In such cases the deceased child should be urged to move on into the light, or to join those who have appeared to escort him. This subject will be treated in more detail in the chapter on death.

Another situation in which a cutting of the ties is advisable is in the case of an abortion or miscarriage. In the case of a miscarriage, there is usually great sadness on the part of the parents at the loss of an expected child and the mother has also suffered a break in her bodily rhythm for which she needs help. The ritual for release is the same as that for parents and children but with the addition of reassurance to the child that it was not rejected in any way because of its premature death.

I find that the mothers are able to let go of a great deal of pent up feeling during such a session and I always urge them to allow tears to flow to wash away their grief. When a miscarriage has occurred they usually have a nagging feeling of guilt that perhaps, in some way, they may themselves have caused it by neglecting to follow the correct diet or exercise regime, by overeating, smoking or drinking; so this is a wonderful opportunity for them to express the often barely admitted guilt and to ask forgiveness of the soul who was denied entry into a human body. Frequently, Christ, Baba, or other numinous figures appear to reassure or forgive them.

In the case of an abortion, the procedure is the same. However, since the decision to reject the incoming soul was a deliberate act on the part of the woman, it is very important for her to ask forgiveness from whoever would have been born to her as a result of the unwanted pregnancy. The relief of the mother is often overwhelming after being given the opportunity to experience forgiveness for her act of rejection. Without this relief, some women carry guilt with them for years.

Some attempted abortions are unsuccessful and can affect the soul seeking entry into the world as the baby. I recall two cases which illustrate this situation in which the mother took steps to bring about an abortion and failed. In one case, drugs were used and, in the other a metal hook. Both children, one a female and the other a male, had expressed resentment and anger towards the mother for no apparent reason and, in addition, had an overpowering fear of rejection. It was not until each one discovered the underlying cause for their attitudes and the old trauma was unearthed and the mother had been forgiven, that the abnormal fears of rejection gradually subsided and a more positive relationship with the mother was possible.

## Cutting Ties from Other Family Members

In some families where there are many children, the older ones are often expected to take responsibility for the younger ones who may, as a result, feel as if they have more than one mother and father. This can be very confusing to a child as he develops. In such a situation, it is necessary to take the person through a ritual to detach him from the older siblings as if they were his parents, in order to free him to discover his own identity.

We have also seen instances of such a strong bond between a brother and sister that it prevents either of them from sustaining a successful relationship with another man or woman. I do not intend to suggest that all such close relationships are necessarily incestuous, although in some cases this may actually be true; even when not overtly expressed, incestuous feelings may be present but are suppressed due to cultural taboos.

Sometimes it is so deeply hidden that the two people are completely unconscious of it and would be outraged if it were brought to their attention even though it may be obvious to other people who know them. We usually uncover such attachments when we are first discussing the members of the family group in order to determine which ones have most influenced or programmed the person seeking release.

I recall one woman who had had two marriages, both of which had ended in divorce, caused by her habit of frequently quoting her older brother to her husband and taking her brother's side in any discussion between the two men. When she finally saw the situation and understood its underlying cause, she was willing to go through the process of detaching from her brother. She then really worked to discover her own inner animus, and was eventually able, for the first time, to relate fully to a man. She has remarried and this time, apparently, she is happy.

Sometimes such a close bond can prevent one or both siblings from attempting marriage because of a vague and uneasy feeling that it would be disloyal to the beloved brother or sister. Some people fear that they could never have such a good relationship with anyone else.

There are also negative relationships between children of the same parents in which there is an unreasoning dislike or hate for one another. Such a bond, though negative, is just as constricting as a positive one, and should be cut. It has been made very clear to us that any tight and binding ties, whether they be forged by love or hate, are a hindrance to freedom and self-evolvement and therefore should be faced and handled.

The list of restricting bonds is endless as it includes any two people who have had a close relationship in which one person has strongly affected the other, especially during childhood when the mind is so impressionable. Many such close relationships, we have discovered, have their beginnings back in a past life in which the two people may have been together before but in a different relationship to one another. For instance the wife now, might have been the husband before; a brother and sister in this life, and lovers or man and wife before; and so on. If this appears to be a possibility, then it is advisable to try to tap into the prior life to learn more about the former relationships, with the purpose of understanding them and learning how best to relate to one another in the present life, and to detach from the past pattern. However, it appears that some groups often reincarnate together, which would explain why members of some families often seem to have especially strong bonds from birth.

## Cutting Ties From Old Relationships

Before a new intimate relationship between a man and woman can be fully successful, all old ties to former partners should be cut to clear the way for a new union to take place and to allow release from all projections of parts of the self on to the former partners.

The ritual is similar to the one already outlined for severing the ties binding parents and children.

First, the Figure Eight must be practised to withdraw all projections so that each person is free from any aspects of the other. Then the cords are visualized, cut, removed and disposed of, and thanks is given to the former partner for all the learning and insight which has resulted from the relationship. Then the ritual of forgiving and asking for forgiveness follows. This is very important, especially where there has been a great deal of friction or ill-feeling between the two people, as in a divorce.

In the case of a woman, an additional cleansing should be performed as we have been shown that a woman actually receives, as if in a container, the essence of each man with whom she has had sexual relations. She should, therefore, remove anything she was retaining before she can be really free to make a clear contact with another man. The process is the same whether the original partner has died or a divorce has separated them or, in the case of cohabitation, if the two have parted in order to go their separate ways.

A good illustration is the case of a young woman who had indulged in many sexual relationships but had subsequently made a decision to leave her old way of life and to follow a spiritual path. She felt a desire to enter into a lasting marriage bond with a man who held the same beliefs as those she was starting to investigate. She felt great love for him but felt soiled by her many earlier alliances and was loath to marry him. Burdened by this heavy load and feeling unworthy of his love, she came to me with her problem. She was overjoyed to hear that there was a way by which she could be cleared and made ready for her new role as a wife.

I directed her to visualize the ties to as many of her former partners as she could remember, and to picture them as hollow straws or pipes attached to the pubic area on each man's body and joined to her at the same area on her own body. She was able to imagine this very easily, so I told her to breathe very deeply and, with each exhalation, to let go of anything she might still be harbouring from the various men, expelling it with force or a deep sigh. With each inhalation, she was directed to visualize golden light pouring into her to cleanse, relax, heal and regenerate whatever part of her needed such treatment. She then asked forgiveness from each man and forgave them all, and ended by thanking them for all she had learned from each, as well as for this period of her life.

I then asked her if she would like to ask forgiveness from her own High C, to which she eagerly agreed. So I suggested that she ask for a symbol or personification of it to appear so that she could communicate with it more easily and feel as if she were really in contact with her own High Self. She had been brought up as a Catholic but had discontinued her beliefs, so she was profoundly surprised and moved to see a beautiful female figure, who reminded her of the Virgin Mary, smiling at her with compassion and love.

She started to cry quietly, and was only barely able to describe how she was taken by this figure to a small waterfall, where she removed her clothes, put on a thin shift and was told to step under the flowing water as if it were a shower, and wash herself thoroughly, letting the cool water run over her entire body. When she came out, the Mother Mary made the mark of the cross on her forehead, and disappeared, leaving her still crying softly, not from sadness but from the deepest relief and gratitude.

She then told this experience to the man who wanted to marry her, and shortly thereafter they were married and had a lovely little baby girl. The young woman is radiantly happy in her new role, free from the heavy load which used to bow her down and make her feel unworthy of love.

We have used variations on this theme many times, with slight changes of detail, each session resulting in release from the past and freedom for the person to move into a new relationship without the tattered remains of the old ones getting in the way.

There is also the problem which faces a person who is still attached to a mate who has died or broken the partnership and who finds it difficult to let go, causing much unnecessary unhappiness. This situation usually occurs when one of the partners has leaned too heavily on the other during their life together, instead of trying to develop his own strength and self-confidence. As a result, he feels abandoned and utterly lost and helpless after his loss.

In extreme cases the bereft partner may lose his hold on life and die to join the other in death. Others report that they feel that the deceased partner is pulling them over to be reunited in death. Some succumb to this pull, but others resist it and want to continue to live. In such cases, we have to make contact with the one who has died, and explain that he must be willing to pass from the earth plane and proceed to other dimensions, and that his living partner will be able to follow him only when it is time for him to die and that no one has the right to bring this about prematurely. More on this subject will be explained in the chapter on death; it is being cited here only in connection with cutting from an old relationship to make room for a new one.

Sometimes we have seen cases where the dead mate will appear in dreams or seems to be in the room, causing the living partner to become very upset or to feel guilty at entertaining the idea of another mate. Obviously, this could be a hindrance to leading a normal life.

There are many reports of people having heard of someone who forgot and called a new mate by the name of the old one, and many people also report that they feel they are making love to the former partner while they are physically involved with the new one. Still others have described that the first mate seems to be trying to intervene between the new couple. One man said that he was sure that his first wife, who had died several years earlier, was in bed with him and his new wife, which made him feel guilty and often incapable of continuing with the love-making to his present wife's bewilderment, and his own embarrassment. In many cases, the surviving mate feels guilty at being with another love partner, and is greatly relieved to be guided through the ceremony of separation from the former mate, the results of which are often quite dramatic.

As can be seen from the above situations, it is so much better if two people release each other within the marriage or close relationship so that each one may become a whole person rather than leaning on the other for support or security. Support and security should be sought within from the High C.

### Cutting Ties For Other People

As I have mentioned earlier, sometimes a person finds it

impossible to slip into the altered state of consciousness which is necessary in order for the conscious mind to be temporarily set aside allowing the subconscious mind to be free from surveillance to present the appropriate pictures or symbols with which to work.

In other cases, the one seeking help may be so insecure that he would not trust his own pictures, and even if he were able to see them would doubt their validity or dub them figments of his imagination. In either case the pictures would not only be invalidated, but doubt would be thrown on the whole process, which would prevent the person from receiving help.

Another situation we encounter quite often involves a person living at a distance who has heard of our work and would like to take advantage of it, but cannot make the journey to work directly and has no one near with whom to work in this way. There are also those who are too young, or too sick to work themselves, or whose situation is so upsetting and so emotionally involved, that it would be impossible for them to relax sufficiently to be open to direction to allow the impressions to break through.

In all such cases, we offer to ask the High C if we should work for them. But before we do this we must have their permission as we have learned never to intrude into the inner life of another person without being requested to do so either directly, or by a parent or guardian in the case of young children, or by a close relative or friend in the case of a critically sick or mentally ill person.

One of the very first times we worked in this way was at the request of an old friend of mine who had had several experiences working directly with me and knew the nature of our work and methods. At the time, he was in England where he and his mother had often visited while she was still alive. England was a much loved country for both of them and this particular visit was the first since her death.

I received an S.O.S. from him by airmail letter telling me that he was having a very difficult time and was in a deep depression and feeling oppressed by memories of his mother. When I first met him he had been tied to his mother and completely under the domination of this extraordinarily strong matriarch and he unwittingly summed up the situation one day shortly after we met. We had been discussing the various concepts of God and, looking at me seriously and in complete innocence of the implications of what he was about to say, he assured me that he had no need of any other God since his mother was his God. Since that time, he had worked hard to extricate himself from her stranglehold which was why he was shattered to discover when he returned to England that she seemed to have moved in on him again as strong as ever. He begged me to see if there was anything I could do to help him.

I immediately called one of the friends with whom I worked for others, and we were instructed in the method of cutting the ties between two absent people for the first time. We have used it ever since then to free many people from the tight bonds which were restricting their growth.

In this case, we had a very hard time convincing the mother that she should let go of her son. She had been not only a strong and wilful woman during her long life, but one who loved life and the excitement of new adventures, challenges and enterprises. She was a very dynamic woman and had lead a very independent life, particularly for her time; We saw that she was still trying to participate in life vicariously through her son, and that when he arrived in England, a country which she had loved so deeply, her presence became overwhelming to him and he sank into a deep depression.

We talked to her as if she were still alive and tried to persuade her of the futility of this half-life she was pursuing when she could move on and into a full life on a different plane, or level of consciousness. We explained that by insisting on remaining here she not only stultified her own growth and evolvement, but also that of her son. She had always held deep religious beliefs so she finally listened and we were able to reason with her.

We discovered that she was frustrated over her inability to enjoy life with her former gusto, even through her son, and that she was ready for any help we could offer her to improve her lot. We were able to help her to turn away from the earth scene, where she had been so powerful, and to face the new way of life awaiting her in another dimension. As we gently, but firmly, urged her forward, she caught sight of her beloved mother and father and described how they were reaching out their hands to help her the rest of the way. Our last glimpse of her was of a radiant woman running to greet her parents. She finally made the transition, and I immediately wrote to my friend describing what we had experienced. However, before he could have received my letter I received one from him telling me that he knew I had answered his plea for help as the oppressive presence of his mother was no longer burdening him. His depression had lifted and he was able to enjoy this visit to England. Later, we checked the date and time when we worked with the time he began to feel free, and found that they coincided. He felt release just as we had finished the session, which was at eleven a.m. our time and seven p.m. in England. My friend had no subsequent experiences of his mother overpowering him thereafter. He was able to let go of his old reactions to her, such as worship, pretended love, and hate, and finally experienced a new kind of love and appreciation made possible by his forgiveness of her for the octopus-hold she had on him.

Not every case works out this quickly. Some take days, weeks, months, and as long as a year before the result can be felt. We learned not to be concerned with the time it takes, but to remain detached from the results and be content to do only what we are shown to do and to leave the outcome to the High C and the person involved. To do otherwise would lead to an ego trip, which we must avoid at all costs.

Chapter 11

# RELEASING
# FROM
# NEGATIVE FORCES

## Negative Powers Used by Groups and Individuals

There have been many prophecies and warnings that in the
Aquarian Age, which we are now approaching, there will be a
confrontation between opposing positive and negative forces, both
on the macrocosmic or world scale and on the microcosmic or
individual level.

From time to time, we have been asked to help people who
have been deluded by an individual or group into believing that
they were being introduced to a positive activity or way of life, only
to discover later, as they were drawn further into it that the exact
opposite was the case. This often seems to happen to good but
naive people who are unaware that there are negative forces in the
world as well as positive ones, and that not everyone has the same
motives or beliefs that they have. When such a person realizes what
has happened to him, he is usually helplessly under the power of a
group or individual and incapable of extricating himself from the
situation without help.

When we are asked to work on such cases, we are shown
protective measures to take to prevent us from being drawn into

the same dilemma. These usually involve some form of light symbol, such as the cylinder, sphere or pyramid, which are described in detail in the chapter on symbols. These usually supply sufficient protection, but there have been times when we have had to visualize putting on armour or using some other equally effective symbolic device in addition to a special protective ritual.

Once we were working to release a man from a group of people who were trying to gain control over him. In the middle of the session we both started to get drowsy and it became increasingly difficult to concentrate on what we were being shown to do. We quickly consulted the High C and realized that some of the members of the group suspected that their victim had asked for help as they had warned him against doing so.

We were shown to make the symbol of the five-pointed star, which is described in the chapter on symbols, at each of the doors and windows of the room where we were working. We also lit sticks of incense and candles, all of which have proved effective in deterring anything of a negative nature from intruding. We were then able to go back and continue the work, both of us wide awake and with no further interference.

Sometimes in such situations we visualize the Figure Eight with the negative group of individuals in one circle and their victim in the other; we then ask to be shown what we can do to bring about a release of the person being overpowered. We have been given different ways of achieving this, each one fitting perfectly the situation on which we are working. However, this part of the work should be undertaken only by those who are absolutely obedient to the inner direction, and only when they are directed to do so from the High C, which usually is not until they have been working for other people for some time.

## Inherited Family Clouds

Over the years we have been shown that certain families carry with them a black cloud, which seems to be composed of all the traumatic experiences suffered by groups or individuals who have at some time been members of that family. This problem is more prevalent in certain ethnic groups. Those groups which we have found to be most affected in this way are Jews, Negroes, Irish and American Indians, since they have all had a history of persecution. It appears that when a member of such a family experiences a certain difficulty in his life, it often triggers the family memory of a similar problem, which results in the person being overwhelmed by his family's old trauma in addition to his own personal trauma, which makes it almost impossible for him to handle it. We have learned to suspect such a possibility in people who are literally overwhelmed by a problem which, on the surface, does not appear to be sufficiently heavy to create such a devastating affect. Many suicides are probably caused in this way.

The first time a family cloud was brought to our attention was when we had been asked to help a young woman who was deeply depressed over a pending divorce and the possibility of losing custody of the children of the marriage. She was distraught and fearful out of all proportion to the seriousness of her plight which, when she was questioned carefully, turned out to be far less dire than she had at first indicated. We undertook to try to find a solution for her in preference to working directly with her, as she was in no condition to participate. We learned from the friends who had asked us to help her that she was not ordinarily an hysterical type of woman and that it was only in this one situation that she seemed to lose control and be so overwhelmed that she was helpless to make some rather obvious and simple decisions regarding her situation.

As soon as the two of us who had undertaken to work for her were relaxed and had gone through the usual preliminaries, I was taken back in time and, at first, concluded that I was being shown one of the woman's past lives. As the picture unfolded, we were able to piece together a bloodcurdling story of the exploits of an Italian family very similar to, but not as famous as the Medicis. I was directed to concentrate in more detail on one particular branch of the family in which a situation similar in many ways to the one in which the woman was involved in her present life had occurred. The children of one family were being bartered back and forth like pawns between two warring sides as if they were merely dolls or puppets rather than human beings with feelings. Little interest was shown in whether they lived or were killed in the fracas. Still thinking it was a past life, I asked what the woman was to learn from her present situation which she had not understood or put into practice in the past one. To our surprise, I learned that the scene I had been witnessing was not of a past life but was part of her own family history and had occurred many generations back. The old experience had been filled with negative emotion which had lingered on as a black cloud over the family ever since. She had unwittingly tuned into it in her present similar situation, which made her seemingly exaggerated reactions understandable and her terror at the thought that her children were in great danger less groundless.

Our next question was what could be done to free her from this old frightening family memory. We were then given a method to disperse the black cloud hanging over the family, which would relieve not only the woman for whom we were working but any other members of the family who might trigger this old memory as she had done. We have used this same method for many black clouds over families or ethnic groups.

## To Disperse a Black Cloud

Two people, or more if available, should sit quietly with eyes closed and reach up in imagination to the sun with arms outstretched and hands together with palms up to form a cup in which to receive from the sun whatever positive force or energy is needed to disperse or dissolve the negative emotions in the cloud. When those participating feel filled with this solar energy they lower their arms and place their hands with palms together and fingers straight as if in prayer and direct the energy into the visualized cloud from their finger tips until it begins to thin out and eventually disappears.

One young man with whom I worked to disperse his family cloud was able to describe how it slowly changed from dark grey to grey with yellow streaks, then to pale grey and, finally, to a thick white mist which disappeared as he watched us pointing our closed hands at it to direct into it the healing energy we had received from the sun.

It is particularly fulfilling to be able to dissipate these black clouds from the world. It is also encouraging to hear that the overpowering gloom, fear, or other negative emotions have lifted from the person asking for help, leaving only his own personal problem to be dealt with. Often we are told that other members of the family also feel in some way freer.

I have been asked what such a cloud feels like and can only give as an example that strange uncomfortable feeling sometimes experienced in certain houses or cities where, with no knowledge of the reason, there is an urgent need to get away as fast as possible before becoming immersed in depression.

## The Inherited Ink Blot

A child born into a family draws from a reservoir of genes which carry both positive and negative family patterns. The process can be likened to a computer that receives information about the traits and weaknesses the new family member needs for his learning in this life. Those patterns not needed at this particular time remain dormant or latent in the subconscious.

Unlike the black cloud, which is triggered when a personal trauma coincides with an old family problem, a negative inherited pattern, which we call the ink blot, is already present in the baby from the time of birth. It can take the form of negative tendencies, emotions or traits on any level of the person. The family black cloud is attracted from outside the person, whereas the ink blot is within him from the very beginning.

If a person has been working conscientiously on the negative aspects of himself, and is aware of the lessons to be learned from them, the process can be accelerated and the negative patterns lessened. To accomplish this, an ink blot is visualized by the person. As soon as it appears on his inner screen he should shine a beam of light on it, which will gradually lighten it so that it can be more easily dealt with in a later session. This exercise should be practised once every day for at least a week, and longer, if necessary. The length of time is determined by the speed with which the blot is dispelled by the light. When this has been accomplished and the blot has lost its black colouring, the person can be taken into a wak-ing dream session in which he can ask to be shown what else needs to be done to erase it completely from his personality.

My daughter saw that her ink blot was like a dark muddy pool which dried up as she shone the light on it each day. At the end of a week the original area was outlined in black, so that it was still faintly visible. When she asked to be shown what she should do now, she was prompted to take a spade and dig up the earth all around the space. When she had done this she decided to plant seeds of the opposite traits to replace the ink blot.

Each person discovers his own method of dealing with his ink blot when it has been seen clearly. Sometimes the ritual is long and elaborate, while others prefer to make it quick and simple. As with all the other techniques, it should be accomplished by the person himself, as he is the best one to beam the message of its removal to his own subconscious.

Chapter 12

# THE INNER ENEMY

Another figure which is usually very elusive, often showing up fleetingly in dreams or reveries, must be dealt with before a person can be free to follow his own path towards wholeness. We call this figure The Inner Enemy. It is a composite of all the aspects of a person which constantly work against him and his best interests, however conscientiously he may try to make progress in any pursuit. It assumes many shapes and can be male or female, young or old. Its appearance heralds a breakthrough to the core of a particular problem, often the most central one. A great deal of energy is usually tied up in The Inner Enemy which, when it is dealt with, is released for use in daily living. But more important, this additional energy can help to accelerate growth towards wholeness.

The Inner Enemy is the source of many nightmares, taking the form of killer, attacker, tempter, seducer, doubter, mocker, or any other form which prevents the person from reaching his goal.

Everyone has pockets of negativity hidden within them, many of which are brought over from former incarnations. They have to become conscious before they can be seen clearly and cleaned out. However, if they erupt too quickly or suddenly, the person can be inundated by the contents of his unconscious. If they happen to be too heavy or frightening for him to face and handle, he may seek to escape by withdrawing into amnesia or insanity, by becoming seriously ill often to the point of death, by committing suicide, becoming an alcoholic or drug addict, or by hundreds of other ways man has devised to escape pain. Therefore, it is dangerous to seek this figure before it appears spontaneously, perhaps in a dream, for to do so can open up a veritable pandora's box. When these negative figures appear spontaneously in dreams it is an indication that the person is ready to deal with them. Only after one has appeared do we ask the High C to indicate the appropriate way in which we should cautiously proceed so that the person is faced with only as much as he can handle at any particular time.

As in the work to separate a person from anything or anyone, we first give him the Figure Eight exercise, which is used in this case to isolate the character in the dream which symbolizes the part of himself which threatens him in any way. The next step is to cut the connecting ties visualized between him and his Inner Enemy using the standard technique and asking to be shown what should be done with the negative figure. Sometimes it is possible to salvage it in the same manner as the child within. Often just seeing it in the opposite circle of the Figure Eight is sufficient to reduce its size and power. But in some cases it is so threatening that it must first be rendered powerless and then dealt with in an appropriate way.

I recall one young man's dream in which a figure appeared who was responsible for sabotaging everything he ever attempted to do. He used the Figure Eight and in the following session he was startled to see that his Inner Enemy had changed and become a sick sniveling beggar. We both asked that he be shown what to do with that part of himself. He was shocked at the quick inner response that he must step on it and squeeze out all the energy trapped in this beggarly part of himself. He hesitated so I suggested that he check again and this time he had the distinct impression that the beggar himself was entreating him to act quickly and put him out of his misery. That must have struck a sympathetic cord in him for he was able to proceed, discovering as he did so that the figure which had been so threatening, crumpled beneath his foot as if made of *papier mache'* and was easily reduced to dust, which he swept up in a dustpan and threw into a fire.

Another young man uncovered his Inner Enemy while we were invoking his Cosmic Parents. He could see him as a stony adolescent bent on destroying him and preventing him from making contact with his Cosmic Parents. However, this first confrontation was not the right time to do more than bring this negative figure out into the open where he stayed until we could work again, causing all kinds of problems in the poor man's life in the interim of several weeks.

At the next meeting, as soon as he was relaxed, he reported that he could see the boy and that he was as threatening as before in spite of his efforts to try to tame him. I suggested that he call on his Cosmic Father to give him the necessary strength with which to deal with this situation. I then had a sudden impulse to suggest that he engage the boy in a boxing match. He tried this and was amazed to see that at his approach the boy became frightened, weak and cowardly, and he was able to knock him out with a quick blow at the solar plexus.

He then asked me, "What do you want me to do with him, kill him?", to which I replied, "I don't know what you should do. Ask your High C to show you." He then proceeded to describe how he took the cowering boy by one arm, held him high in the air, swung him around his head, and flung him into outer space. With the boy out of the way, we were able to complete the connection with the Cosmic Parents.

When the dream introducing the Inner Enemy takes on nightmare proportions, we have to be open to the possibility that the figure has attracted to it an overlay of other negative thought forms on the same wave length or vibration causing it to appear terrifyingly overpowering to the dreamer. To handle such a figure, we need the help of the person's authority figure, Cosmic Father, or other appropriate archetype to supply the additional strength and energy needed to vanquish the foe.

We have observed that this negative figure frequently surfaces to consciousness when a person has made a serious commitment to follow a path or method towards self-knowledge and development. The Inner Enemy is intent on preventing him from this positive move which, naturally, threatens its power to hold sway within him. This is one of the causes for so many seemingly negative experiences occurring in a person's life as soon as he starts to work on himself in a positive way.

### Removing Other Negative Thought Forms

In addition to the Inner Enemy in human form, other negative facets that cause problems can occur within people and must be dealt with in order to free the real self. They also frequently surface from the subconscious in a dream, which is an indication that the person is ready to handle them. They should not be sought without a definite inner indication that the time is right for such a quest.

Sometimes they take the form of animals and are ancient remains of our original animal nature. In a recent talk, Baba elaborated upon this point. He likened various tendencies in people to certain animals, pointing out that these attributes are still active in people. He said that the buffalo is known for its willfulness, pride and self-conceit. The sheep's main characteristic is foolishness, which prevents it from being open to reasoning or persuasion. The cat is known for its thieving and slyness and for appropriating to itself what it cannot get by direct means. The monkey is wayward and unsteady, always jumping from one tree to another. The list could be extended to include many others, such as the pig symbolizing greed, the rhinoceros vicious attack. Each person should ask to be shown his own symbols and their interpretations. These can often be recognized in a person by his behaviour and, once faced and admitted, can be dealt with in many different ways. The most common method is to lure them out into the open and set them free to return to their natural habitat, sending them on their way with a blessing.

There are some people who actually feel something heavy or gnawing in a particular part of their body and sometimes associate it with a specific emotion such as fear, anger, or guilt. In such cases it is not always possible for them to remove it themselves as it may have become a part of them, in which case it must be operated on just as a tumour or other growth needs to be cut out of a physical body.

There are two ways of doing this. If the one working with the person who has the problem is sufficiently experienced and is also shown by the High C to undertake the task, he can perform the operation to remove the unwanted aspect by following the inner guidance from the High C to direct him. Another method is for two people who have had experience in working together for others to operate to remove the offending object from the afflicted person.

Once when my daughter and I were working for one of her clients who was suffering from anguish, we were shown that the dead embryo of a former dream or creative endeavour needed to be removed. As we proceeded with the operation, she reported that she could actually feel pressure as we worked at a spot below her solar plexus and slightly above her navel.

Another case is that of a young boy who said that he could always feel something in his stomach, which he called Mr Stomach. He was able to draw a picture of it, a very strange looking creature. At his request we were able to remove it from him.

Some illnesses can also be dealt with in a similar way by having the sick person ask to be shown a symbol of the illness in a dream or session. It is fascinating to observe the tremendous variety of such symbols and the different methods people use to destroy them. usually with very positive results.

Problems involving negative symbols within a person have been discussed but some people have a very different type of problem. Instead of harbouring inside them various unwelcome 'guests', they themselves have been overshadowed by negative thought forms or archetypes and are equally hampered and unable to express their real selves. Jonah and the whale is a clear example of this condition. It is usually caused when a person is faced with a situation from which he tries to withdraw and run away, only to be imprisoned in negative emotions such as fear or cowardice.

An example is the case of a man who reacted to his very smothering mother by escaping into books, thus effectively walling himself off from her. In so doing, he imprisoned himself in his own world, which was symbolized in a dream as a sea monster. He dreamed that he was inside this creature as it swam in the ocean. He was incapable of extricating himself or destroying his prison. Here was a typical example of a situation where the rescue would have to be effected by the person conducting the session, in this case, myself. I was shown that the creature must be brought up out of the sea and on to dry land before it would be safe to rescue the man imprisoned inside it; if not, he would be in danger of being 'set adrift in the ocean of the unconscious. I had to use a harpoon and, remembering the instructions in the book, *Zen in the Art of Archery* by Herrigel. I asked for the harpoon to be released at the right time and aimed at a vulnerable spot on the creature's body to avoid hurting the man trapped inside. As soon as this was accomplished, the dying sea monster had to be pulled ashore, where an incision could be made in its body through which the man could emerge. As soon as he was released, he helped to push the monster back into the ocean. He was then free, on firm ground and ready to take the necessary further steps to become fully conscious.

We have learned that life must be faced for there is no permanent escape, and, in the long run, it is more satisfying to deal with a situation than to try and avoid it perpetually. We have also been shown that drink, drugs, cigarettes, even meditation, indeed anything which is used as an escape, all have the effect of either opening the users to negative thought forms or of sealing them off from life in an unreal world of their own. In both cases the users are out of contact with life and other people. All of these conditions are products of the ego, which is the most difficult aspect of a person to control. It is snake-like; it slithers on to the scene unexpectedly and often unrecognized, to trick one into relying on its own dictates rather than on those of the High C. Its hold can only be chipped away gradually, as the person becomes willing to surrender more and more of himself to the direction of the High C. He cannot kill his own ego, but it can be starved into submission if he stops feeding its insatiable hunger for dominance over hint.

Chapter 13

# THE INNER HOUSE

After the separation from the parents and guardians, a person will often dream of a house. In dreams or reveries, a house often symbolizes the structure which a person has built up around himself to delineate the territory or space which he occupies in his world, where he lives and moves and has his being.

A dream can give an insight into the condition of a person's Inner House and can indicate the next steps he should take towards discovering his true self. The dream can show him what he needs to do to make the house more to his liking. It would be preferable if people would set their own house in order before telling someone else what to do.

A person will often dream of being back in a house where he lived as a child. This is a sign that he is still living back in that old childhood setting and that some part of him is still at the age he was when he lived there. To help him to correct this situation and bring it up-to-date, we take him back in to the dream as if it were a reverie. We then direct him first to find a more suitable house which more nearly represents his present adult life and then to bring his Inner Child out of the old setting and into the new one where he can start to help it to grow into maturity.

Even when there is no dream to point the way, it is wise for a person to investigate his Inner House. At some point in the work, we ask the High C to lead him to a house which represents his present self. The variety of houses discovered in this way is tremendous and fascinating, each one revealing a person's condition and showing him where changes would be desirable.

As soon as he sees his house on the inner scene we take the subject on a tour of it, first outside and then inside, and encourage him to verbalize what he sees and to comment on his reactions. Sometimes he will voluntarily decide that changes should be made, in which case we encourage him to make them as soon as he sees the need. He may report that his house has no windows or that the window shades are drawn and the whole house or certain rooms are dark. Obviously it is not difficult to conclude that this person is closed within himself and does not want to look outside of himself or have anyone look in at him. If such is the situation, he is encouraged to open up the shades to allow the light to enter and then clean and air out and repair any part of the house which he feels is in need of attention.

Occasionally a room will be locked, most often the basement which symbolizes the subconscious. If such is the case, it may take a whole session to lead the person gently but firmly to unlock the door to the closed area within himself and to face whatever has been kept hidden from his conscious mind. Many old forgotten traumas, guilts and negative memories come to light in this way. If a great deal of fear wells up at the thought of unlocking a closed door, we ask for a personification of the High Self to appear to accompany him and to help him face and deal with whatever he finds within.

After his house has been opened up and cleaned, we suggest that he now change or redecorate it in whatever way appeals to him, by making any structural changes he sees fit and by erasing old worn out parts and replacing them with new ones. We always stress that it may be a long time before it appears completely satisfactory to him but that he can and should make any changes he wishes, and as often as he wishes, until he feels it is more to his liking and comfort. Quite often a person will prefer to work on one room at a time. He may choose to start with the kitchen, which is where food is prepared and therefore where nourishment is provided. Other rooms often needing attention are the bathroom, where elimination of waste or unusable matter and cleansing take place; the basement, where memories from the past are stored and may need to be taken out and looked at; and the bedroom where he is closest to his unconscious during sleep.

We also suggest that each person arrange for a place in his house, either a room or a corner of a room, however small, where he can go to meditate and where he can practise the various mental exercises he needs to do from time to time. This area should be planned very carefully. It should be quiet and simply decorated with the minimum of furniture to avoid distraction. Some people choose to include an altar, others prefer to use pictures or figures of an inspirational character, or a candle or some other symbolic object. As soon as he has completed it, we recommend that the person go mentally to this place before starting either meditation or visual exercises so that his mental atmosphere will be conducive to a state of peace and awareness.

It is interesting to see the changes which take place in people as they work on themselves by changing their Inner House. One of the most common reactions is delight at the freedom to decorate the house in exactly the way they wish. Most people are obliged to consider the tastes of those with whom they live, and some are still under the influence of their parents' or even grandparents' tastes.

I recall working with one young girl in her late twenties who dreamed of an old-fashioned house, Victorian in style, containing very heavy dark furniture and heavy draperies almost covering the windows. Everything was in perfect order but she felt cramped and frightened as she looked around. I began questioning her to try to uncover the reason why she was dreaming of such an old-fashioned house and discovered that she had lived with her maternal grandparents between the ages of five and eight years. When asked to describe them, she related that her grandmother, in particular, had very Victorian tastes, ideas, customs and attitudes which the grandmother had instilled into her as a little girl during the years she lived with her. She realized that she was still being affected by this early programming and that it restricted her in many undesirable ways and made it very difficult for her to fit comfortably with her peers, who often excluded her because of her old-fashioned attitudes.

When she saw clearly what had happened, she threw herself enthusiastically into the task of building her very own house from the ground up. As she did so, it helped her to let go of some of the old outmoded beliefs with which she had felt weighted down. She has continued this process in her daily life.

Sometimes a dream or reverie will bring to light a house which looks very attractive from the outside but, once inside, is a mess. It is a shock to the person who sees such a picture as it shows that he puts on a good face but is not always as attractive beneath the veneer. There are as many different houses as there are people who are willing to find them and work with them to change themselves.

For some people, a garden also presents a way by which they can work on themselves by using the various flowers and trees to symbolize useful and positive habits or abilities in themselves, and the weeds to represent their negative or destructive traits. An excellent daily visual exercise consists of planting one flower to represent a desired quality or ability, and up-rooting one weed to symbolize one fault or unwanted habit.

One young girl to whom I suggested this exercise was most excited about it and really worked hard in her garden and reported from time to time how she watered and tended the plants each day. One day, to her amazement, a figure of Christ appeared in her inner garden and talked to her. He continued to appear each day for several weeks to teach her many things about herself which gave her invaluable insights. Each person uses this exercise differently. It is, however, the effect on him which is important, so we urge him to feel free to use it in whatever way will help him the most.

Chapter 14

# THE MANDALA

It is important for each person to work on achieving a balance of the four functions of intuition, sensation, feeling or emotion, and intellect or thinking. I will now describe one of the exercises we have been given to help achieve this balance. We call this exercise the *mandala,* and it was first given for use by my own family, which was comprised of my husband, myself and our two daughters.

One Christmas vacation, when both daughters were home from school, the older one, who had recently started to work with me, asked if I would go within and see if the four of us could be given help and instruction to develop a more harmonious family relationship. We all had very different strong personalities which made it difficult to avoid clashes when we were all together for any length of time. It was especially difficult this vacation because the girls had been away at school for several years and had enjoyed their independence.

This was the first of several such sessions which have helped us all to meet many crises as a family and have encouraged us to join together to seek the right solution for all of us as a group rather than one of us dominating the others, or all four insisting on a different idea or plan. However, this method is one of the hardest ones to use and it often takes a long time before each person is really willing to seek a common solution instead of insisting on his own. Later we have found that the *Mandala* can be used by anyone to help him to balance his four functions which is necessary before he can become whole or integrated.

As soon as I had become quiet and had slipped into the reverie or waking-dream state, I saw a large sphere at eye level in front of me which looked like the moon with the sun shining behind it. It was divided into eight pie-shaped segments and, as I watched, each alternate one was filled in with a different colour. In the centre, a small diamond reflecting all the colours appeared. The coloured sections formed a cross. The one at the top was yellow, the one at the bottom green, the right-hand one blue, and the one on the left a deep rose colour.

It was then shown that this symbol represented the balanced or whole person, a goal towards which we are all evolving. I was shown that we, like the moon, can reflect the light of the sun through these four coloured lenses, which represent the four main functions of intuition, sensation, thinking and feeling through which we make contact with the world around us.

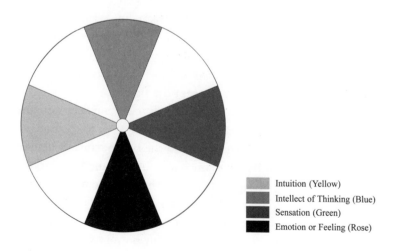

Intuition (Yellow)
Intellect of Thinking (Blue)
Sensation (Green)
Emotion or Feeling (Rose)

**THE MANDALA**

I noticed that the coloured parts fell into the general shape of a human body, the yellow at the top representing the head, the green at the bottom the feet, the blue on the right side the right arm, and the rose on the left side the left arm. Then I was shown that the yellow, or head, stood for intuition; the green, or feet, for sensation; the blue, or right arm for thinking; and the rose, or left arm, for feeling. In the figure which I was first shown, all four colours were of the same strength, indicating that the four functions were equally developed. However, this is a rare exception seen only in a master who has practised one of the *yogas* or other disciplines and has achieved perfect balance.

I was then shown for each family member which functions were weak and which were strong. Next I was instructed to imagine I could reach behind each colour and locate a rheostat which, when turned to the right, would intensify the colour and when turned to the left would lower the intensity. Usually one function has been developed beyond and at the expense of the other three. To remedy this imbalance, the rheostat behind the over-developed one needs to be turned down a little, while the weakest one has to be turned up and the other two raised or lowered accordingly.

In most people, one function is dominant, one is almost entirely lacking or buried in the subconscious and therefore of little use, and the other two lie somewhere in between. To illustrate this imbalance I was told to stand erect with arms outstretched to my sides so that my body would represent the figure.

First I was shown how it would appear if the intellect were the strongest of the four functions. I bent my body over to the right so that the arm pointed to the ground and the other arm was held in the air. I could see and feel how my whole body leaned over to the right, throwing it out of alignment. Likewise, if the emotions were the strongest, I would be weighted down on the left side, throwing my body off balance in the opposite direction. If the intuition were the strongest, the sensation would probably be very weak; I would not be sufficiently grounded and would be floating ten feet off the ground, suspended in the air. If sensation were the strongest I would be immersed in tangible things through my five senses of sight, hearing, touch, taste and smell, and I would probably be closed to intuition or genuinely afraid of it.

When one function is dominant, the person tends to use it more than any of the others simply because it works so well and gives him a sense of security in his ability to function in the world. Perhaps one of the clearest examples of this is a man with an over-developed intellect who uses it in all of his dealings. It is a great help to him in his profession and in business deals, but when it comes to human relationships, particularly in close family situations, it can become a problem and cause much suffering to others especially if his feeling function is absent. In the majority of such cases, instead of developing their inner anima, and therefore their feeling faculty, such men force their wives to carry their feeling function for them. If she happens to be heavy on her feeling side and weaker on the side of the intellect, the couple can lock together and neither of them develops the opposite balancing factor, or weak function. Many couples continue to live in this warped fashion, each leaning on the other as a crutch. When one of the partners is heavy on intuition and the other on sensation, the former will leave to the more practical partner all of the mundane details of living, preferring to live in a dream world rather than to learn to deal with these worldly chores; while the other will attend to the practical aspect of life but neglect to develop the intuitive side.

To help those who sincerely desire to work towards developing all four functions equally, we suggest the practice of a daily routine visualizing the *mandala*. First one visualizes the perfectly balanced *mandala* with all four colours of equal strength, with the sun behind lighting them up. This image should be held for a short time, about two minutes. The next step is to visualize the symbol with the dominant function showing as a very strong colour, the weakest one very pale and the other two somewhere between. It is surprising to see how easy it is for most people to see their own pattern and it is even easier for mates to recognize it in each other. Next the rheostat behind the weakest function would be turned up and the one behind the strongest colour turned down. This new image should be concentrated on for a minute or two.

It is best to start working with the strongest and weakest functions, adding the other two after a change has had time to take place in the person's life. A few seconds of concentration on the original picture, with all the colours at equal strength, completes the exercise. The perfectly balanced symbol, which is the eventual goal, is thus held over as a pattern towards which to work. The whole exercise should last not more than five minutes, which is enough time to beam the message to the subconscious that a change should be initiated. This is a very potent exercise if it is practised regularly on a daily basis. We have heard of some quite startling changes taking place in those who are disciplined and sincere in using it.

As with all the other exercises we have been given, it should be practised as soon after awakening as possible and again just before releasing into sleep at night for the best results. At both of these times the conscious mind is less active and the images can reach past its censorship and drop into the subconscious where the actual work has to take place for a lasting change to be possible.

If a husband and wife are both willing to work on the *mandala* their marriage relationship will flow more smoothly and become a more balanced and active partnership. It will also help them to help each other to develop their weak functions instead of each relying only on their own strong functions, and on the strong ones of the partner instead of developing their own weak functions. The *mandala* can help to correct the common situation in which each person is a leaning post or crutch for the other causing an unhealthy inter-dependence. It is interesting to observe a couple working in this way, for each one is usually far more aware of the other's strong and weak functions than of their own. If they can accept each other's observations, the partnership can become much more meaningful and mutually helpful and dynamic. We are usually too close to see ourselves clearly as we appear to others, but those with whom we live intimately usually know us very well and can be of immeasurable help. But this is only possible if they each have a loving concern for the other's growth, and do not grasp the opportunity to criticize, compete, or 'get back' at each other. If, in addition, they are willing to erect the triangle between them and ask for direction from the

High C, the whole relationship will be raised to a higher level, which in turn will accelerate the evolution of each.

It is helpful to have something tangible to act as a reminder while working on this exercise. The use of the colours, which symbolize the various functions, is excellent for this purpose. It is interesting to see how a person's favourite colour is often the one that symbolizes his dominant function. Thus a very intellectual man woman invariably chooses blue, while the more feeling types will lean towards pink, rose and red.

Now that it has become fashionable and socially acceptable for men to wear bright colours, a pink shirt could remind a man who has an over-developed intellect that he also needs to develop his feeling side in order to be a better balanced person. A very strong animus-dominated career woman whose thinking function is very strong, could also benefit from wearing pink. On the other hand, overly emotional men or woman can wear blue to remind them to balance their feelings with their intellect. The same technique applies to yellow and green. The dreamy, absent-minded type of man or woman can benefit by wearing more green to ground them in the everyday world of reality, whereas more materialistic people would do well to wear more yellow as a reminder to allow the intuition to be developed to balance their strong sensation level.

Single people who have no mate with whom to confer or practise can enlist the help of a close friend who will be honest and caring. It is very easy to slip into an unbalanced state without being aware of it and this is particularly true of career women. They often become over-aggressive and mere thinking machines. In their fierce competition with men, they tend to rely primarily on their intellect to carry them through and suppress their feminine aspects, which could otherwise act as a balancing factor.

A person who is heavily immersed in his sensations, and who evaluates everything in terms of what his five senses tell him, should be taken on an imaginary flight as a bird. First, we suggest that he visualize any bird, a seagull being a favourite choice for most people perhaps due to the success of Richard Bach's charming book, *Jonathan Livingston Seagull*. He is then directed to watch it in his memory or mind's eye as it flies, swoops, dives into the water, finds a wind current and lazily rides on it letting the wind carry it along without even the need to use its wings to fly. Then we suggest that he identify with the bird, imagine himself rising into the air, and playing 'follow the leader' as he probably did as a child, copying every move the bird makes. He should be encouraged to describe everything that is happening, how it feels and what he sees, to help him to experience fully the freedom of flying. For many people this is such a new experience that they find it hard to let go of the security of their contact with the earth, but as they become more deeply involved in the exercise, a sense of exhilaration and wonder replaces the misgivings and insecurity, and they usually end up thoroughly enjoying the exercise.

This bird exercise is not advisable for a person who is heavily developed on the opposite pole of intuition as this type tends to fly too much already. So, we take him on a very different imaginary trip. First we suggest that he visualize putting on heavy green boots, which may even need to be weighted to hold him firmly on the ground. He is then directed to take a walk along a path which will open up ahead of him. It may be a country road, busy street, a path towards a beach or some other trail. The important point is for him to keep both feet firmly on the ground all the time and resist the temptation to start flying above the ground. In extreme cases this may prove to be very difficult. Changing a pattern of many years standing is not an easy task to undertake. The wonderfully free sense of flying and being barely in touch with the earth is very hard for some people to relinquish and they complain that the alternate path of sensation is too slow and plodding. This contrast is one of the major problems faced by those who have indulged heavily in the use of hallucinatory drugs and it is the reason that so many of them remain 'hooked'. Drugs can be disastrous for people whose strong function is intuition as they can lead to their death by giving them a false belief that they can actually fly. Drugs can cause them to be cut off from so-called reality so that they remain perpetually in an unnatural dimension of consciousness without the use of the other three functions t balance them. Mental hospitals are full of such people.

We also suggest that this type of intuitive person try to conscious use their five senses more each day in order to open themselves to fuller awareness of all that is taking place in the world around them. Some type of physical activity is also useful to make the more aware of the physical body in which they live. It is only through the body that they can make contact with the world an the people in it in order to work out their *karma*.

Another symbol, a step pyramid, was offered as an extra aid for balancing the four functions. Each of the four sides of the figure represents a function and is coloured appropriately. When it first appeared in a session, I was shown that every person is at a different step up from the ground on each of the four walls of the pyramid For instance, one person might be twenty steps up the blue side for intellect, twelve steps up the green wall of sensation, five steps the yellow wall for intuition and, perhaps only on the first or lower step of the rose side for feeling. This is a very clear to see where a person is in relation to the four functions and it can be used as a variation from the *mandala*. To use the pyramid, a person is directed to go in his imagination inside the pyramid and to stand in the centre of it immediately under the point of the roof and to face the side representing his weakest function. He is then told to open himself as fully as possible to absorb the colour, looking at it in imagination, remembering seeing it, or actually looking at it on a piece of paper or cloth of that colour. He is then told to take a deep breath and feel as if he is literally breathing in all that the colour symbolizes.

One young girl asked if, like Alice in Wonderland, she could break off a piece of it and eat it. My answer was that she should do whatever came to her mind which might help her to make the exercise more real for her and thus ensure that the message reached her subconscious mind.

The next step in the visualization is to ask the person to turn and face their next weakest function, and so on around the four sides of the pyramid, allowing about fifteen breaths for the weakest, ten for the next weakest, five for the next and one big breath for the strongest one.

The maypole, which is described in the chapter on symbols, can also be used in a similar way by asking a person to visualize holding a ribbon in the colour of his weakest function. While holding it, he is directed to open up as fully as possible to receive from the top of the maypole, representing the High C, the qualities comprising the function he needs. He changes ribbons to work in this way with each of the other functions.

## Crystals

We often use rock crystal as a tool to bring about a better balance in a person. Quartz crystal is naturally polarized, that is, it contains both positive and negative poles and so can be used like a receiving set, as in the early radios or crystal sets. Rock crystals have been used for centuries as protective devices, divining stones, for meditation, and for healing, and they are reputed to stimulate latent intuitive abilities in sensitive people. Crystals can be worn around the neck for protection or held as meditation pieces in the palm of the left hand with the right hand covering it to complete the circuit between the hands. Most people prefer to own one which can be used as a piece of jewellery and doubles as a meditation talisman.

As soon as the crystal has been chosen, we ask that it be cleansed and that an appropriate meditation be given for the new owner, as well as instructions as to the best place on the body for it to be worn.

In meditation each crystal is offered up to Nut, the Egyptian Goddess of the sky, who reputedly steers the departing souls across the dividing line between this world and the next. The crystal is left in her care for three days. When it is retrieved, it has been cleansed and imbued with the qualities of the owner's High C and he is given a meditation to use with the stone. The meditations are invariably most appropriate and, when practised daily with the crystal, have proved to be helpful.

Chapter15

# DREAMS AND WHAT THEY MEAN

I have repeatedly referred to the role dreams play in this work and will now explain in detail how we use them. When a person first calls for an appointment, having been referred by someone who has already experienced the work, he usually needs help with a specific problem or else wishes to work on himself to achieve balance and integration. After deciding on a time to meet, I ask him to watch for any dreams he may have from that night until he arrives for our first meeting. I request that he write out the dreams in as much detail as possible because they can show us where to start working.

Very frequently a new person will report having a very vivid dream just prior to our first meeting. It is as if the subconscious, in anticipation, grasps the opportunity to send a message through to the conscious mind now that help with the translation is at hand. Some people tell me that they never dream, in which case I explain that everyone dreams, even those who have no conscious memory of having done so. Most people can train themselves to remember their dreams and to write them down or tape them. It is very important to record the dream because so often a person awakens during the night having just experienced a dream and lies in bed reviewing it, even interpreting it. Being so sure that he could not possibly forget it, he goes back to sleep without recording it and, to his chagrin, finds that he cannot recall even a small detail when he reawakens.

It is a good idea to keep a small pad of paper, a pen or pencil and a tiny flashlight by the bedside within easy reach to make it a very simple matter to write down any dreams which are clear enough to wake up the dreamer. Some people prefer to use a tape recorder and find they are able to turn the machine on, speak into it, and switch it off again whenever they awaken with a dream and then slip back into sleep. However, if they are taped, the dreams must be transcribed later so that they can be interpreted.

Because dreams come from the unconscious, the dreamer knows on some level the meaning of his own dreams and can therefore learn their common symbols and be helped to understand the messages from this hidden part of his own mind. When dreams seem to elude interpretation by the conscious mind, we ask for their meaning by means of the reverie technique. After the person is relaxed and we have asked for help from the High C in deciphering the dream, I often take the dreamer back into the dream and have him relive it and ask the meaning as it unfolds. Using this method, it is often possible for him to understand the message and to make changes in the dream while reliving it. If he is involved in running away from an attacker he can, rather than continue to run, turn around and face whoever is pursuing him. At times it can come as a shock to discover the identity of the one giving chase.

One young woman gasped as she turned to face her pursuer and blurted out, "It is me. I am chasing myself!" She realized how true this was in her daily life as she was always rushing breathlessly as if afraid she might never reach her destination on time.

Another woman, on turning to face her pursuer, was stunned to find that there was not one person but three following her: her husband and her parents. She sobbed as she understood what this meant, for she knew immediately how well it fitted her life. From infancy she had always been hurried along by her parents in everything she ever did, always feeling that she was too little to keep up with them. She married a man who made her feel the same way, unconsciously choosing a familiar though painful pattern, as people so often do. I directed her to face the trio and to talk calmly to them, telling them that she had her own inner time clock and rhythm and that she was, from then on, going to obey it instead of them. I suggested that she use the Figure Eight around each one of her pursuers to stop their intrusion into her territory. She promised to follow through with this exercise but assured me that just understanding what the dream was telling her, and seeing how she was constantly reacting to her family, removed a lot of pressure from her.

Frequently, a person will awaken before a dream has ended which can leave him feeling high and dry and even panicked. I have often heard someone say, "And just at that point, I awoke so I don't know what was going to happen next, and I feel terrible as I can't get it out of my mind." This feeling can be resolved into deep relief when the person is led back into the dream and encouraged to finish it.

But a most important fact for our work is that dreams often indicate where a person should start in the work and frequently lead straight to the main problem. For example, one woman presented a dream fragment that was only one sentence long and she was thoroughly disgusted that she could not remember more of it. Her father had given her a bunch of red roses which had many more thorns than usual. When she eagerly grabbed the roses her hands were torn. I suggested to her that her main problem was with her father and that we should begin our work by cutting the ties to her father. She was amazed that I was right and added that her other main problem is her relationships with men. She gets love but always with many thorns.

We have been shown to regard dreams as small plays or scenes from plays presented by the unconscious mind to instruct the dreamer about himself. Some dreams show the dreamer his fears or desires. Some compensate for areas that are out of balance and some show the dreamer the future. It is as if each of the characters inner scenes acts out a facet of the dreamer's personality. Each person contains within him a whole troupe of performers, some of whom co-operate together while others demand to have own way and pull the others off balance. These varied facets of the personality show up in dreams personified both by people know in daily life and by strangers we do not recognize.

In Order to analyze the roles played by the actors in the dream plays, I suggest that the dreamer should describe each of the people he recognizes and determine what each one symbolizes. Then he can understand the part played by that facet of himself in his life, as well as that played by the actual people. Dreams play an invaluable role in showing the dreamer that other people, both in dreams and in waking life, can be used as mirrors in which can be seen reflections of his own inner facets. These projections challenge him to discriminate between the facets in himself he admires and those he would like to change or eradicate. Having seen facets of himself in others in this way, he can begin to take responsibility for his own faults instead of criticizing them in others.

The unrecognized actors in the dream represent hidden or unconscious facets of the dreamer's psyche. It is their behaviour in the dream that gives clues about unconscious traits in the dreamer.

For a man, the male characters, whether known or unknown, personify the various parts of his masculine, thinking self and the women will represent the various qualities of his feminine or feeling side, the anima. For the woman, the female dream figures will represent aspects of her feminine self and the male actors, aspects of her male within or animus.

The dreamer's next task is to review this inner group of players and to watch as he catches glimpses of them interacting in his daily life. He must eventually bring them all under conscious control, the females forming a united feminine side of himself and the males uniting into one masculine side. When all of the disparate and sometimes warring parts have been brought together and united into two main figures, these will show up consistently for a while in dreams. Finally the dreamer will dream of an inner marriage between them. When the inner wife or husband is found within the dreamer, he or she will be better able to stop projecting his own inner attributes on to his mate or love partner.

The child of this inner union, or mystical marriage, will represent the new, whole, balanced self. Until its birth, which often occurs in a dream, this new self has only been glimpsed as a potentiality. As it matures and develops, the inner child will eventually be able to replace the fractured person who had been pulled in many different directions by all the separate facets.

The child of the inner marriage will be seen in dreams as a numinous, precocious or very special child, while ordinary babies and children in dreams represent newly developing or recently acquired facets of the personality. Sometimes, however, a child will represent a personality facet that has been stuck or fixated at a young age indicating that the dreamer must work to mature this part of himself.

Occasionally the characters appearing in dreams will have a special aura, will be larger than life, or extraordinary in some way. These will often represent archetypes such as the wise old man or Cosmic Father, the wise old woman or Cosmic Mother, the Inner Enemy and other symbols described earlier. Dreams can alert the dreamer to danger of possession or vulnerability to negative influences by outside people or forces. Nightmares are often warnings of this type or clues to the Inner Enemy.

It is very important to watch dreams to determine the effects of the work and visualizations on the dreamer. The subconscious mind will comment on the progress of the work through dreams and will invariably show what needs to be done and when.

I have worked with myriads of dreams and believe the following examples will help illustrate the work.

A homosexual male with whom I had worked many times had a dream which I will give in full, along with the work we did together to unlock its meaning.

"I was walking down a sidewalk with my hands and arms filled with many packages. I came to a group of women and one man who were playing volley-ball, but without a net.

The ball got away, and bounced towards me. They waited for me to throw it back. I tried a couple of times but was unsuccessful, since my hands and arms were holding the packages. Finally, I managed to use my knee to send it back. I thought I had done well to get it back to them at all under the circumstances.

They went on playing, but seemed a little derisive. As I got closer the man threw me a much smaller, dingy red rubber ball, not bright red like the other. I was surprised and angry because he had not given me any warning, or chance to catch it. I put down my parcels and threw it back to him. He caught it and passed it on to the woman. Then he mimicked the way I had thrown it, with a limp wrist. I was hurt, embarrassed, very angry and upset to think that my gayness was so obvious and sissy-like that he would do that to me."

When I asked him if he had any idea what the packages contained, which were hampering him from playing ball with other parts of which as represented by the group of women and man, he said he had no idea, but would very much like to find out.

So I relaxed him into the reverie state and suggested that he ask his High Self to show him what he was carrying around with him which was preventing him from becoming involved in the game of life and what he should do about it.

He discovered that there were seven packages, which he proceeded to open one at a time. He described the contents and asked to have them explained.

The first one contained a stuffed doll which was mostly head with very little body. He said it reminded him of his grandfather with a moustache like his, and it was a cuddly doll. As he looked at it, he understood that he had copied certain traits of this grandfather, which he now decided that he did not want any more. He burst out, "I don't want that part of me any more, so I am going to put it back on a shelf in a store."

When he opened the second package. a punching puppet was revealed. Again, he spoke with feeling, "It is made out of black crazy-quilting, and is very, very ugly, like a caricature. I don't like it. It is a part of me which accepted anything and everything from everyone. I must destroy it. So I cut it up, and with a big mallet smashed it against a rock; burned what was left, and blew away the ashes."

The next package held a beach ball striped in red, white and blue and green sections with gold thread connecting them.

"It represents other peoples' promises which I have inflated and kept to play with. First I must deflate the ball. It collapses like a balloon and there's not much left of it. It looks like a soggy old thing now. I cut it up with scissors, dig a hole in the earth and bury it so that it will mould away".

Next came a steam-iron which was very heavy. "It symbolizes the way I always try to smooth everything out first before I attempt to do anything. No more stiff starch and no more iron! I throw it in the ocean, and it is so heavy that it made a big splash and went to the bottom."

The fifth package held a clear plastic box, inside which was a valentine made of waxy rice paper decorated in red and white, with a love note printed on it. "It symbolizes nostalgia for past loves and hopes. I burn it. It is very delicate so it catches fire quickly. I throw the box into the fire too."

In the next package he found a gold bread-basket lined in red velvet in which was a pair of binoculars with feminine eyes painted on the lenses.

"I see out from a feminine point of view, but it is surface without depth or feeling. I don't want to look out through those binoculars any more, so I throw them into a volcano, and watch as the lava melts them. I find a new pair of binoculars with nothing painted on them. I can adjust them to female or male vision. I wear them around my neck within easy reach when I need them. I keep the bread-basket inside me which feels good."

The last package held a very tiny box which contained a perfume bottle. "It is very pretty and sparkles like a crystal, but I don't like the smell so I can't keep it as the scent has soaked into the crystal. It symbolizes old crystallized emotions. They are too sweet and sticky. I throw it into the volcano."

Another young man who is a devotee of Sai Baba had a dream in which Baba represented his own High Self and gave him advice. Here it is:

"I am standing in what looks like the main street in a Western town around the time of the 1800's with wooden houses and stores and a dirt street. There are Sai Baba devotees seated in front of one of the buildings awaiting Baba. I have just arrived and feel we should be sitting somewhere else. While I am standing there debating whether to go and sit where I think we should, or join the others, or maybe tell them my thoughts, Baba appears and walks past me. I ask him where to sit and he points to the spot I had felt was right. I then ask him this question in regard to my personal life and my difficulty in making decisions, "Baba, do you really take care of every little detail or just the really important decisions?" He replied, "I don't bother with the details. You have been given two hands with which to create your material life. You get what you deserve. The same holds true on the spiritual planes.'"

This dream was so clear, and answered his question so precisely that it needed no further interpretation.

Another very clear message was presented in the following dream to a young woman who has great difficulty with self-discipline.

She dreamed that she and her mother and an unknown man were standing at the top of a long incline or flight of stairs which they were about to descend. As she looked ahead she was most surprised to see that the path was covered as with a carpet with French pastries. She wondered if she should walk on them and decided that it would not be a good idea, but her mother assured her that it would be all right so she allowed herself to be persuaded and they started to walk down, at which point she awoke feeling very strange.

As French pastries symbolize, to most people, a form of self-indulgence, the dream was apparently telling her that if she took this path she would be walking downhill into self-indulgence.

Her conscious self knew this and was ready to decide against going that way. But the pattern laid down by her mother in childhood was still operating within her at a deep unconscious level, luring her into the old pattern.

To help her to work with this problem we had to examine her early programming so that she could see where the problem originated, and then decide how to replace the negative pattern with a more positive one.

As an example of how a person who is familiar with the technique can receive messages from the subconscious through dreams, I am including a series of very helpful dreams I had one year when my husband and I were on a visit to Japan. At the time I was having various physical ailments.

In the first dream I was talking to my mother-in-law on the telephone asking her if she wanted me to order more medicine from a herbal doctor to whom we had taken her recently. She refused the offer, saying that she had her own doctor, whom she could call every day and as often each day as she needed.

She was always on the phone all day, so I interpreted it that I should be in constant communication with my own inner personal healer, and discontinue the herbal remedies I had recently been taking.

From then on, I talked to this inner doctor as if I were on the phone, asking him to take over and heal me of the food poisoning I had at the time, as I did not know how to cure myself. It was a real fight. I would begin to doubt and get worried each time I began to feel ill, but I kept it up during the rest of the trip with variations as I had more dreams.

In the next dream I paid a visit to our family doctor who is an internist. I went to his office for a routine check-up. He examined me and told me that there was a new cure which he explained in detail but which I could not remember upon awakening, except that it had something to do with my eyes. He said he would start treatments right away. I remember thinking how odd it was that he had not mentioned it when I had been to see him only a short time before, but thought that the cure might be so new that he had not known about it then.

We left his office together holding hands very affectionately and walked to where I had parked my car. He was going to give me the treatment in my own home.

I could not find my car, so together we looked all around, and finally discovered that it had been moved. It was stuck in a deep rut. As soon as we got to it to move it, three very rough types of men moved ahead of us, jeering at us, obviously about to wreck the car.

The doctor ordered them off, and got in himself to drive. I suggested that perhaps I should drive as I was more familiar with the car, but he said "No", that he would drive as he had to pull it out of the rut, which would take more strength than I had.

This dream seemed to stem from my having been fighting the first one for several days. Here, the inner doctor was personified by our internist who was one of the most conscientious and dedicated doctors, on call literally any time day or night. He therefore represented one of the most reliable persons I knew.

Now, he was not only going to treat me with a new method, but would also get my car (my way through life) out of the rut it was in, and in addition disperse the three rough intruders who were about to wreck it. These were obviously parts of myself who were bent on deterring me on my path. In the dream I still tried to take over, but he insisted that he should drive which made me realize that I must leave the entire treatment to him and not try to take over myself, or try to get out of the rut with my own conscious mind. After this dream I would talk to this more specific doctor each day.

The very next night I dreamed about a doctor friend of ours who, besides being an excellent doctor, is also involved in psychic research and unorthodox methods of healing. In the dream he was being called in as an extra specialist to work with the internist. They seemed to work very well together and I was pleased about the partnership, which I instinctively felt would be a good one. From then on I added him to my daily inner phone calls for help.

The next night I dreamed that an English psychiatrist whom we had met came from a very long distance to visit me. He was very affectionate, which greatly surprised me as he was a most awe-inspiring Harley Street specialist, with great dignity; hardly a demonstrative type. He told me that he would come any time I needed him, and later sent me a letter confirming it. I was extremely impressed that he would take so much trouble to come from so great a distance to visit me.

He represents a traditional doctor who specialized in psychiatry but was also very interested in mystic and psychic healing and headed a group for the study of different kinds of healing methods in England. One of his books is called *Cure or Heal?* In the dream I knew that he would heal me and not merely cure my symptoms. So he too was added to the list of inner doctors to whom I talked each day.

Then came a dream in which I was with a family consisting of the two parents and several children of various ages. I was immediately aware of a little girl of about eight or nine years of age who was obviously terribly afraid of illness. I recognized that her parents were responsible for her extreme fear, so I took her by the hand and told her that there were many doctors available who could not only cure her of all she might ever have wrong with her, but who were always on hand to help her with any illness which might develop; that if she would come with me I would see that she was taken to these doctors. I knew that her parents had made her afraid, and that it was my responsibility to reassure her that help was available and that she need never be afraid again.

This dream came some time after I had been talking to the inner doctors, calling on them by name and asking them to take over the necessary healing. But I was still going through periods of doubt and fear, the identical apprehension which I remember so well my mother always exhibited. Like her, I was still fearful that I would get sick again, which was extremely difficult to cope with while on a trip.

So I added talking to the little girl each day, reassuring her that she had been taken away from the negative influence of her parents. As I interpreted this dream I saw that a part of me which was symbolized by the little girl was still very much afraid, and had not really believed the prior dreams and so was pulling in the opposite direction when I worked with the various doctor parts of myself. She must be reassured by me consciously so that she too would begin to believe in them, which would dispel her apprehension. After this dream I finally began to make headway.

Not long after, I dreamed that I had had a most remarkable baby, which I did not seem to know anything about, as it had been cared for until then by a nurse. As I watched the nurse tend it, I realized that, though she was very efficient, she really did not know the best routine for this baby. Only I knew how best to care for it, and that I myself must now take over its complete care, as I knew just what to feed it and how to handle it. I immediately took it away from the nurse and put it on a routine which I knew it needed in order to thrive and grow.

I interpreted this dream that the baby personified a very new growth within me since I had started to work with the inner doctors, but that I must now consciously take responsibility for its care myself, and not leave it to the nurse or unconscious part of me.

Chapter 16

# CORRIDOR OF DOORS

At times in a reverie a person will report that he is walking down along an endless corridor with doors on either side, but does not know which door to enter. We have been shown how to use this device to unearth old traumas, fears, rejection, frustration, loneliness and many other problems of unknown origin. It can also help a person to explore himself.

After the relaxation exercise, we direct the person to visualize a long corridor, such as those in large office buildings, with doors along each side. We explain that each door will have a sign on it, such as fear, guilt, jealousy, love, loneliness and other emotions. If the person's problem is fear, we suggest that he walk down the corridor looking at the various doors until he comes to the one marked fear. At this point, particularly with fear, we often ask if he would like to call on one of the authority figures to accompany him through the door so that he can see what lies behind it. Then he is directed to look carefully to see how the door opens whether by means of a knob, a latch, a key, or by some other method. Most people find this quite easy to do as it delays the actual opening of the door which many people subconsciously are afraid to do. Even when a helping figure accompanies the one about to enter the door, he must be willing to take the actual steps, and do whatever is indicated himself as his own mental and emotional muscles need to be strengthened. The only way to achieve this is to make the effort himself. Once the door is open and the person is willing to step over the thresh hold, a wide variety of scenes may await him. The area behind the door does not always turn out to be a room but can lead to diverse, strange and, often, faraway places.

The role of the helper or partner in this visualization is to keep plying the person with questions to encourage him to give a detailed description of what he sees and how he feels. He must be assured that somewhere through the door he can find the root cause of his fear, or the answer to whatever question he is asking. It is not at all uncommon for the seeker to block, even though he wants desperately to find the answer. If this occurs he must be distracted and, in some other way, led around the block. Sometimes it is a good idea to have him visualize the block as a stone wall or a mountain and then suggest he find a way through, over, around, or under it. Sometimes the cause is found in an event which occurred during his childhood and has been long forgotten or repressed.

I remember one man who had an unreasoning fear of dark, enclosed places and discovered in a session that the cause lay back in time when he was four years old and was locked in a broom closet by a maid. He heard again the key turn in the lock as the maid walked away leaving him to repent his sins. This grown man started to sob as if his heart would break, which almost prevented him from telling me what he was seeing. Finally, through his tears he outlined the scene he had just witnessed. I asked him to call on a personification of his High Self to appear and help him. He was quiet for a while and finally whispered that he saw a very beautiful figure of a woman who was smiling at him and holding out her hand for him to take. Together they went back into the scene which had so frightened him. They unlocked the closet and rescued the child whom the woman comforted and forgave him for whatever he had done to cause the punishment. He reported that he could gradually feel the old fear being released as he watched the inner scene and accepted the freedom and absolution from guilt which his kindly companion was bestowing on him so generously.

A similar procedure is used for problems of insecurity, rejection, anger, hate, jealousy and many more. Sometimes a problem will not be tied to a specific cause as in the one above, but instead may be a personality trait. In that case, what we refer to as a teaching picture may be seen. This is similar to a dream and when interpreted, will give the clue to handling the problem.

When one young woman who was having a difficult time relating to men, went through a door marked 'Love Relationships', she saw a scene involving a very strident woman berating a man and literally beating him over the head with a yardstick. She was puzzled, so I suggested that first she should try to interpret it as if it were a dream to see if it was showing her something she needed to know about herself. She was very quiet for a long time and finally asked if I thought it was telling her that she mentally bludgeoned men with her quick mind of which she was very proud. I asked her what a ruler or yardstick meant to her and she replied that it measured things. At that she gasped as she realized that she berated a man if he did not 'measure up' to her expectations. She needed to work on her emotional function to balance her very strong intellect so that she could meet men as a woman rather than as another man.

One man was greatly surprised to see a flight of steps descending immediately in front of him as he opened a door marked 'Anger'. I gently urged him to go down one step at a time until he reached the bottom. He followed my directions and found himself in a dark, dank dungeon. He told me that his anger was getting out of control and begged me to bring him back out of the reverie before it overpowered him. I reminded him that he had entered the door marked 'Anger' hoping to find the cause which could very well be right here- in this place and I suggested that he ask to be shown what it was. Everything in him agreed to this he told me, but he was still loath to stay there and very much afraid of what he might be shown.

I diverted his attention by asking him to look down at his feet, hands and body and to describe them to me. He gave a little gasp and in a tone of disbelief reported that he was barefoot and clad in ragged but elegant clothing, reminiscent of the finery worn by men of other times. I continued to question him and he was able to piece together a story of having lived as a nobleman at the time of the French Revolution who was thrown into prison for no offence except that he was wealthy. His anger sprang from the indignation he felt that he, who had been one of the few good masters to his peasants, should be facing the same fate as those who were guilty of oppression. "Where is the justice in this?" he had railed as he languished in the prison. He continued to recount that he was taken to the *guillotine* while filled with these strong negative emotions. As he considered his present situation, he realized that he was still carrying the old anger within him and that it would flare up unexpectedly at the slightest suspicion of unfair treatment towards him.

I directed him to look back and to try to understand the mentality of the majority of peasants who were abused and starving and who were stirred into rebellion by men who knew just how to incite a crowd to mass hysteria which swept away any other thoughts or emotions each person might have had as an individual. He saw that this was exactly what had happened and that his own peasants had lost sight of the fact that he had been good to them as they rallied around new leaders who were promising them food and liberty. I asked him if with this understanding, he could forgive them for what they had done. He agreed and as he did so, he said that he could feel the old anger slip away. and disappear.

The next step was to put this insight into practice in his daily life, so I suggested that he could murmur the word 'peasant' under his breath whenever he felt himself beginning to give vent to anger. He tried this and called me a few days later to tell me that he had thought of a better way, which was to say, "You are dead, Jean-Claude", which was the name with which he referred to the Frenchman of the past.

Obviously there is no rule which can be applied to all situations as it is a matter of guiding each person a step at a time and asking the High C for guidance in determining what questions to ask to help the inner pictures unfold.

Chapter 17

# DEATH AND DEATH RITES

Just as we have lost the major part of the original puberty rites, so we have allowed to drop into disuse the most important part of the death rites, which should be performed prior to death as well as at the actual time of death to prepare the departing soul for moving into the new dimension of consciousness immediately. In our Western culture most people still have such a fear of death that they prefer to ignore it rather than to open their minds to an understanding and acceptance of it as an inevitable part of the cycle which governs this material world in which we live.

In ancient times, there were complicated manuals designed to guide those whose job it was to officiate at the death rites, two of which are still available: *The Tibetan Book of the Dead* and *The Egyptian Book of the Dead*. Some vestiges of the old rituals also remain in the funeral services held in various churches and temples but these, unfortunately, are too often mere shells of the former deeply symbolic and meaningful ceremonies and have very little effect on either the deceased person or on his bereaved relatives and friends. In recent years, however, the whole topic of death and dying has been opened up and finally looked at squarely by many people working in this field.

Unless death is very sudden and unexpected such as from accident, heart attack, massive stroke, or in battle, there are certain signs to alert those attending a sick person of the approach of death at least two weeks before it actually occurs. An old Indian *guru* once described these signs to me, and I will now present them as they are very easy to recognize. About two weeks before death, the patient will start to rub the fingers of both of his hands together from time to time during the day. About a week later, he will start to look up at the ceiling of his room a great deal of the time. At about four days prior to death, he will begin to wipe his face with his hands and complain that he feels as if ants were crawling on it or that cobwebs were clinging to it. At three days, if his face is washed with water, it will dry almost instantly, the skin seeming to absorb the water like blotting paper. One day before the end, he will repeatedly slip down to the end of his bed and continue to do so after an attendant has lifted him back up. Six hours before death he will be shocked to discover that the roof appears to be no longer visible, and around forty-five minutes before the end, his breathing becomes very heavy and laboured, until the death rattle occurs, announcing that death is imminent.

It is just as important for the members of his family to be prepared ahead of time to face this event as it is for the one about to leave his physical body. Their attitude can so affect him that it can make his passing either an easy and peaceful one, or a tearful and sorrowful one. Actually, those who are about to lose the physical presence of a loved one often need help and instruction even more than the sick and dying person. The latter often reaches a point at which he craves a quick release from his pain and suffering, especially after a long illness. He may be willing to let go of his physical body but is held back by the sorrow and reluctance of the living, who are too involved with their own sorrow to understand his need to die and to accept it.

Ideally, both the dying person and his close relatives should already have been taken through the ritual to severe the ties between them. Each member is then free to make his exit from the earth scene undetained either by his relatives or by his own attachments to life. However, it is never too late to introduce this method if the person is willing, and to guide a close relative or friend of the dying person to use the Figure Eight around himself and the one about to die in order to ease the separation for both of them. The ties can then be cut between them to ensure a quick release. If the dying person is sufficiently conscious and wishes to go through a similar ceremony, it can greatly facilitate his passage out of his body with far less fear.

We have learned that it is very important for a person to be fully conscious at death in order to be able to see the bright light which is like a beacon to lead the soul away from the earth scene and into a new dimension. During the period of separation from the body it is most helpful if there is someone present to remind the departing soul to watch for this light and to look for anyone who has already passed on and who may be waiting to help him across to join them.

It is advisable for someone to be in attendance daily with those who have had no prior teaching on death to prepare them for acceptance of their approaching demise. Just as people face life in many different ways, they approach death with a wide variety of attitudes depending on their various attachments to the world scene. The person in attendance should possess a very strong belief that life does not end with the death of the physical body and that the soul, when released from its confines, continues to exist but in a different dimension and in a more subtle body. A deep conviction such as this will greatly affect the one about to make the transition. This service sometimes presents the helper with a real test of his patience and strength of belief. This is especially true if the one about to die is strongly attached to any aspect of earthly life, or has no belief in a continuance of life in any form beyond the grave, and fights to live to the very end.

One such case involved a man who was dying of cancer and had no belief in anything other than what his five senses showed him about this material world. His doctor had, at the onset of the disease, given him three years to live, of which two years still remained, so he was determined to finish out his allotted time. His will was so strong that, weak and emaciated though he was, he clung on to the metal guard rails on the hospital bed as if this would help him to stay in his body. It was unbelievable to those who saw his condition that he would want to remain in that tormented body, but the fear of extinction was greater than his discomfort so he continued to hold on desperately, endeavouring to stay alive at all costs. It took several days of talking to him, repeatedly detaching his hands from the bedrails and telling him of my own certainty that death is not the extinction of a person as he believed it to be, before he would open his mind even a crack to such a possibility. He fought every inch of the way, yet I could sense that from time to time he was slipping in and out of his body. This was also indicated when I took his wife through the ritual to cut the ties between the two of them to help her to release him. She reported that she could see him outside of his body looking well and happy. This helped her to feel much more relaxed about him and helped to prepare her for his physical death. I persevered with such repeated directions as, "Relax!", "Let go", "Float free of your body and you will feel less discomfort", and began to suggest that he look around to see if he could see any of his relatives who had already passed on and who might be there waiting to greet him and help him over into the dimension in which they now lived.

I myself became vividly aware of my own father who had died some years earlier. He frequently appears to help those who need someone to escort them across the line which separates the living and the so-called dead if for some reason there are no familiar relatives or close friends to meet them. I shared with the dying man my feeling of the presence of my father and asked if he would be willing to do me a favour and take a personal message to my father to deliver when they met on the other side. At first he resisted such an idea violently, but I kept repeating it. Quite suddenly, in a very strong voice he said, "Okay, I am ready. Please help me to go." From then on, my task was much easier as I now had his co-operation and he no longer grasped the bedrails but lay quietly, all fight gradually draining out of him. Shortly after this, he slipped into a deep coma and started the recognizable laboured breathing which indicated that he was barely attached to his body which was exhibiting automatic reactions before the final release. I continued to direct him to follow my father as he led him away from his shell of a body and into the light of the world beyond.

A sequel to this story occurred about three years after his death. My daughter and I were working together for people in our usual way. Among the requests for our help was one from a man who asked us if we could check to be sure that his mother had fully passed on beyond the physical level. He had had a very disturbing dream in which he saw her looking horribly ill as when he had last seen her, just before she died several months earlier. He mentioned that she looked lost. He added that, unlike him, she had held no belief in a life after death.

Almost as soon as we had asked for direction from the High C, I was startled to see the man whose death I have just described. He looked jaunty and with his old puckish grin he said, "I have come to tell you that you were right. I am still alive. I didn't believe you when you tried to tell me. Remember how I fought you? I was a real son-of-a-bitch. You worked so hard and I was so rude. I've come now to apologize." Then he asked me to tell his widow that he did love her and was sorry he had been such a 'son-of-a--bitch.' This happened just a few days before his wife's birthday so it was like a beautiful gift to give her this message. Later I realized that he and the woman for whom we were about to work had one thing in common. Neither of them had believed in a life after death during their lifetime.

Another experience was that of a woman who was also in the last stages of cancer, but she had a deep belief in God. She also had a very strong will and was more than ordinarily attached to her children and grandchildren, as well as to her money and possessions. Her daughter and I had already cut the ties connecting her to each member of her family so she was free to leave when the time arrived. She too moved in and out of consciousness and when she was conscious she could talk and would often confide that she did not want to die and was frightened at the prospect of leaving all that was familiar for the unknown. Her will was so strong that she held on to life despite the very obvious approach of the end of her physical energy. She repeatedly moaned that she was terrified at the thoughts of leaving all that she loved, especially her family, and of being alone. She had feared loneliness all of her life and it was the reason why she clung to her children so desperately. I talked to her about release and suggested that she look beyond the objective world to see if she could recognize any of her deceased relatives or friends who might be waiting to greet her. This seemed to distract her and she immediately started to call "Mama, Mama" over and over in the voice of a child and with a childlike smile on her face. She described a large motherly woman whom she said was holding her arms out to her. I encouraged her to run into those welcoming arms as she used to do as a small child and to curl up in that ample lap and feel arms around her, comforting and soothing her and to hear the voice reassuring her that she would never again be lonely. I took it for granted that the woman she described was her mother, but later her daughter informed me that she was very close to her grandmother who had been like a mother to her and whom she had always called Mama. She also told me that the grandmother was a very large and motherly woman, whereas the mother was much thinner and of a rather cold disposition.

From then on the woman slipped back and forth between two states of consciousness, alternately holding on with rebellion at having to die, and calling on her grandmother. It was very hard for her to let go of her extremely strong will, even in the face of death. Finally she gave up the struggle as her bodily functions weakened and slowed down. She lapsed into a coma and died very peacefully a few hours later.

These two cases were unusually difficult ones because of the reluctance of both people to let go. They were each the type of person who could very easily have remained too close to earthly consciousness and caused problems to their families. The majority of people about to die are far less resistant and need only a little help to release willingly and peacefully, frequently with a smile still lingering on their faces at the end. Almost everyone dying is able to see those who are waiting to greet them and the joy they often express at their reunion with loved ones is very touching to behold. In some cases, where no close relatives or friends appear to welcome the dying, there may appear the figures of 'helpers', as we have come to call them, who come as death approaches to help the one who is dying across the invisible line which divides the two worlds. As I mentioned above, my father is one such helper and often appears to escort people across. There are always helpers available to perform this service. But those who are about to depart this life do not always know about them, and therefore cannot take steps to reach them, which are necessary as the helpers can approach this earthly dimension only as far as the dividing line. The dying must be free to move towards that line by following a very bright light which appears to guide them and to reach out so that they can be helped across and into the new element.

I mentioned earlier the difficulties often experienced by those who die suddenly by way of an accident, murder, in battle or when death was completely unexpected and therefore no preparation for it was possible. These people often remain earth-bound after death. These disembodied spirits can cause haunting and other visitations from the dead. *Part* of our work has been directed towards releasing these souls, some of whom do not appear to realize that they are no longer in a physical body and are often frustrated when they cannot attract the attention of the remaining members of their family and friends.

We have often been asked to check to make sure that a loved one has successfully made the passage safely, especially when the death has been sudden or violent. The procedure is for two volunteers to erect the triangle and to ask the High C to take over and direct them. However, this kind of work should be undertaken only by those who are experienced in the reverie technique and who have learned to be obedient to the directions from within. They will therefore have been working in this way for a long time and will be able to slip into the inner waking dream state very quickly and without the need for the preliminary relaxation.

As a team, the two endeavour to make contact with the deceased person by calling him by name. When contact is made they explain to him that he has died and offer to help him to move on to other areas and to join others who have also died. Invariably they are so relieved to find someone who will talk to them and listen to what they want to say that they are eager for any suggestions. But this is not always the case. Some put up a fight to remain on this plane, often in order to stay attached to some member of their family whose energy they are using to enable them to stay close to this physical world. As soon as we have impressed upon them that they are caught in an in-between area and are neither alive in this tangible world nor fully incorporated into the other one, we lead them in the direction of the dividing line and ask them to look ahead and beyond to where it is very light. They are usually startled to see friends in the distance, some of whom they recognize as relatives or friends who have already left the earth scene. Some still refuse to believe what they seem to be seeing. In this case we usually suggest that it is worth a try to find out if what they see is a reality. We tell them that the best way to find out is to move in the direction of these figures and, as they get nearer, to decide whether it is just a mirage or if they are real. Meanwhile the friends and helpers make every effort to attract the attention of the confused soul. Some people report that they see them waving to them, calling them by a pet name and in many other ways reassuring them of their identity.

We can take departing spirits to the dividing line, but no further. They themselves have to be willing to move the rest of the way to where the waiting figures are ready to grasp their hands and help them across into a new way of life. When we see them safely in the hands of helpers, our job is finished. Their new experiences are none of our concern.

Occasionally we will find that the shock of death was so severe and they are still so attached to the body, that the process of releasing them is more complicated. They may need to be healed, bathed in a pool or stream to wash away the frightening memories, or directed to shed the old sick body which they sometimes feel is still around them. I think our work with my mother-in-law illustrates this situation very clearly.

My husband and I were away when we received a cable that his mother had died. In meditation that morning, I saw her slumped in a heap and knew that she had not gone far enough to reach help. I told my husband what I had seen and that we must help her. We both visualized each of us holding one of her arms with our other arms around her back so that we could lift her up and support her. It reminded me of the way she was helped to walk after she suffered a stroke, by holding onto the railing along a wall at the nursing home where she lived. I started talking to her, telling her that we would help her to reach those who were awaiting her on the other side. I could clearly see my own father and, behind him, a group including her deceased husband, her father and mother, and others. She was listless and lacking interest, so I continued to talk to her, but she would slump down again as we tried to help her to move forward. We picked her up again each time she slumped and I was guided to tell her that she would become young and beautiful again when she reached the other side. I pointed out a thin cloud separating us from the group awaiting her. As soon as she heard that she would be young and beautiful again, she aroused herself and looked ahead in the direction I was pointing. Then she straightened up and, as she did so, she shed the old helpless body like a snake shedding its constricting skin, and moved towards the waiting group. We were able to introduce her to my father, who took her hand and led her to the others, some of whom she now recognized with pleasure. She looked back once and waved as if to thank us and, radiantly smiling, moved out of sight.

My husband made the comment that since suffering the stroke which had prevented her from walking without help four years before, she had probably held on to that pattern of helplessness and had acted as if she were still attached to her useless body. She had always been an extremely vain woman and was very proud of her youthful appearance, her beauty and her clothes, so the promise of their return was the one thing which penetrated her lassitude and changed the mistaken belief that she was still attached to her physical body.

Sometimes we find that a spirit is afraid to make the complete crossing because of guilt over something he had done in this life. One such case involved a woman who had died of cancer of the throat. Some months after her death, a close friend asked for help.

She related a series of very strange experiences she had been having. She would feel the presence of the deceased woman in the room with her. She had brushed these feelings aside, thinking that she was just being superstitious. But finally, one day she actually saw her friend's face and heard her say, "You are the only one who can help me. I am having trouble passing over. I still seem to be stuck in this world." The poor friend was really frightened as she had never experienced anything of this kind before and thought she must be going crazy. We assured her that we would try to help and that we would report back to her as soon as we had worked for her friend. As we started to work we saw the woman slumped over and looking forlorn and hopeless. We introduced ourselves as friends of her friend to whom she had appealed for help and told her that we were there to help her. She seemed immediately to be aware of us and fell to her knees with her hands upraised pleading for help. We told her not to kneel down to us and led her into the triangle between us and showed her how to reach up to the apex to the High C, her own High Self, for help.

I then saw a beautiful pale oval face appear at the apex of the triangle. The eyes were extraordinary: compassionate, yet piercing. At first she shrank away from it and I sensed that she was afraid to face this Presence. She had had an abortion when she was in her teens which had prevented her later from having children. Her decision had darkened her whole life with a heavy sense of guilt and now made her afraid to move across into her rightful place. I seemed to be in contact with the face and felt it was directing me to tell her that she was forgiven and had compensated for her youthful folly by dedicating her life to the welfare of many orphaned children. It appeared that her fears were finally outweighed by her misery at being stuck in the *bardo* region, as this in-between area is called in the *Tibetan Book of the Dead*. She seemed to be ready to accept forgiveness and knelt down again with her hands reaching up towards the face, begging for forgiveness and release. I was told that her burden of guilt was not all acquired in this life, but that some of it was brought over from a prior life in Italy. It was, however, not necessary for us to uncover any details about it. We were shown an ascending flight of white marble steps and were told to guide her towards them and to urge her to climb up a step at a time, stopping for a few seconds on each one. This would revive her memory of similar steps which she had once climbed many times to a place where she had been very happy. We were able to persuade her to climb up a step at a time though very slowly, and, as she neared the top, I saw a hand reach down to help her. I could see a lace ruff attached to a dark green velvet sleeve and was told that this was the hand of someone she had known in the Italian life whom she could trust to guide her further. As soon as she caught sight of the hand, she obviously recognized the lace ruff at the wrist and the person to whom it belonged, and hurried up the last steps to meet him. At the top she turned around to thank us for our help before she moved out of sight.

We reported back to her friend who had asked us to work. We have also talked to her several times since, and she has told us that she has never had a recurrence of the strange visitations which had prompted her to ask for help. We feel confident that the woman has left this plane and is wherever she needs to be for further learning.

People who have been exposed to any religious system, invariably see at death the figurehead or originator of their chosen belief system whom they joyfully follow, releasing willingly from their earthly life. Such figures as Jesus, the Madonna, Mohammed, Buddha, one of the saints, or one of the aspects of God from the Indian pantheon may appear to them. When we are shown that the last rites need to be performed for a soul after death, the appropriate figure always appears to officiate.

In one interesting case involving the death of the son of a minister, we had been asked to check to be sure that he had made the passage successfully. As we worked we discovered that he was still in shock from dying suddenly in an accident. Because of this Christian background, we called for Christ to appear but, to my surprise, I saw the huge statue of Christ called Corcovado which stands high on a hill above Rio de Janeiro in Brazil. Puzzled, I asked the reason and was given the impression that this statue symbolized for the boy the aspect of Christ to which he had been exposed as he grew up: huge and overpowering, watching everyone from his high perch and, like a statue, hard, unfeeling and unapproachable. We immediately called on the very different figure of Christ who usually appears to us. He is also very different from the traditional images depicted in paintings and sculptures. He has such power that his approach is felt long before He is near enough to be recognizable in the inner scene. He is very large and strong and has a rough-hewn face which is kind and very beautiful, but not in the conventional sense. We pointed out this approaching figure to the boy who was dazzled by the light surrounding Him as well as by His appearance. It was easy for the boy to follow this figure and, as they moved off together, his face was radiant.

Chapter 18

# SYMBOLS AND HOW TO USE THEM

Over the years, various symbols have been given to us to be used as exercises for specific purposes in a daily routine. The subconscious part of the brain has to be reached and programmed before a new habit can be started. If the learning steps reach only the conscious mind, the knowledge is merely in the head and is soon forgotten. To reach the subconscious, a new piece of information has to be repeated daily many times, preferably in pictorial form, because that part of the mind is not rational and does not understand reasoning or words. This truth has always been known to the old teachers, hence the Chinese saying that a picture is far more useful than a thousand words.

Thus when we flash a symbol or picture daily, the subconscious acts on the comments it receives in this way and co-operates with the conscious mind to bring about the desired effect. After a symbol has been used a number of times, it gathers energy and this, in turn, increases the depth to which the message is imprinted.

Some of the symbols we use have been mentioned earlier in their appropriate place in the text. These include the triangle, Figure Eight. tree, *mandala* and maypole. Others are for specific problems such as guilt, fear, anger, et cetera, while still others are used for protection.

I will describe each one separately, with instructions for its use, to make it easier to find the one most applicable to the particular situation when needed. Some of the symbols should be introduced to the person about to use them after he has been relaxed in the routine manner, while others can be given even over the telephone, which is especially useful in cases of crisis or emergency.

After a time it becomes quite easy to pick the correct symbol for a particular problem, as well as to extend its use to other situations.

## Protective Symbols

Often it is necessary to give a person a specific symbol as a protection from some person or situation which is too strong and powerful for him to deal with until he is able to work in other ways to build up sufficient strength and security in himself to cope with it. We have been given many symbols for this purpose, so we either ask to be shown which one is applicable, or allow the person to pick the one which feels right to him.

### Balloon or Bubble

This is to be visualized exactly like a soap bubble, reflecting from its surface all the colours of the rainbow, but less fragile, and more like a rubber balloon, though large enough for the person using it to be able to move around comfortably inside it. It is especially helpful for super-sensitive persons who react to the slightest criticism, real or imagined, as the barbs bounce off the surface of the bubble and cannot affect them. We find that most people accept the symbol with real enthusiasm and immediately feel safer when they imagine it to be around them at arm's length in all directions.

As this is a thought form, we explain that it is possible to keep it in place in the imagination wherever the person happens to be, in a group of people, driving a car, in the midst of traffic, or flying in a plane. There is therefore no excuse for not doing the exercise. We advocate using it as often as needed, until the person is strong enough to handle those situations and relationships which usually disturb him.

## Plate Glass Screen

Sometimes when a person comes for help, it becomes apparent that a certain relationship, most often with a negative parent, is so threatening that it is difficult for him even to be willing to do the Figure Eight, preparatory to cutting the ties that bind him to this person. Other relationships which often present this difficulty are those with in-laws, other relatives, a boss, workmates, etc.

For such extreme reactions we use an imaginary, very thick shatterproof glass screen, which is visualized between the person and whoever is the problem he has to deal with. The Figure Eight may then be practised with the screen erected at the place where the two circles join, so that each person is effectively separated from the other.

This is usually a temporary protection, but is most effective when it is used, as it allows the person to relax until he develops sufficient strength to deal with the problem without this crutch, as further insight makes this possible.

## Cylinder of Light

This symbol has been suggested as a protection for someone who feels that life is very threatening for some reason and temporarily needs to be insulated in order to work on the causes of this condition.

First, we suggest that a circle of gold light be imagined or visualized on the ground at arm's length around him. As soon as this is clearly seen, we direct him to draw the gold light up from the circle to form a cylinder of light all around him, from his feet all the way up above his head, or as far as he wishes it to be, for comfort and security.

As with the other devices, this should be visualized in the morning and kept in place throughout the day by remembering to be aware of it at intervals during the day. It should be visualized again on retiring for sleep, to insure the continued feeling of security throughout the night, when people feel most vulnerable.

## The Pyramid

This symbol was given originally as an extra aid in balancing the four functions, but it is also often used as a protective device. In this case, the person imagines that he is standing in the centre inside the pyramid, just beneath the apex, and visualizes light flowing down from that point as from the High C, and filling the entire space. Several of those to whom it has been given have reported an increase of energy after using it, in addition to the protection. Another way to use the pyramid to help balance the four functions has been described in detail at the end of the chapter on the *mandala* on page 108. It can be referred to for use in this way.

### Umbrella or Sunshade

This is often suggested for a person who feels his head is in a whirl caused by people bombarding him with their opinions, demands, criticisms, and doubts, so that he finds it difficult to be sure of what he himself really thinks about something, and therefore has trouble making decisions.

He is told to imagine the central shaft of the umbrella running up his spine and on up through his head like an antenna, with the canopy the same size as the circle used to designate each person's territory, that is, at arm's length around him. As with the other symbols, it is a matter of remembering to be aware of it and keeping it in place at all times. It can be discarded as soon as the person has become strong enough to withstand other peoples' demands and commands.

The central pole can be imagined connecting him up to his own High C, the canopy screening out distraction, so that he can begin to catch the quiet messages which emanate from that point to help him to decide what to do and in which direction to move.

I once asked Sai Baba how we could differentiate between our own will, the strong will of another person, such as that of a parent or—mate, and that of our High C. He answered, "When you are in doubt, do nothing. Then go to a quiet place and ask to be shown, and you will know." Using the umbrella helps to do this more easily.

### Scales

A symbol we were given to help with decision making is a pair of scales. This visualization is more easily done with the help of another person, in the form of a mini-reverie. As soon as the person is relaxed and the triangle has been visualized, the one seeking help is instructed to imagine, or remember a large pair of scales with a centre pole and two arms at either side suspended from which are two pans or trays. We then suggest that he place on one of the trays a symbol for one of the two possible solutions, and a symbol for the other solution on the other tray. He is then told to turn away from his inner scene for a few moments, then turn back quickly, look at the scales, and immediately say which pan is weighted down lower than the other.

Some people report that the two pans are moving up and down, so we direct them to watch until they finally stop, then they will be able to see which one is lower and which is higher. Others see one higher and the other lower almost immediately, and very quickly realize that the heavier side is the more favourable choice. or holds more weight as a solution. Sometimes both pans are evenly balanced, which suggests that either decision would be acceptable.

### Crossroads

Another symbol we often use for decision making is a cross-roads with various signposts indicating different directions. The person who is at a crossroads in life is asked to visualize this symbol and read what is written on the signs. Often one will say 'Dead-end', another, 'Detour', while others will bear a specific direction which is understood by the person, or he will see a symbol which can be interpreted. Sometimes it is necessary for him to be willing to go down one or more of the paths to find out where each one will lead before a decision can be reached. Many people who have used this method are amazed that such a simple way works so well in finding answers to their questions.

### Five-Pointed Star

Sometimes we are asked for a protection against psychic invasion of various kinds. For this we have been given a five-pointed star or pentacle, which is a very old symbol with a long history of many uses. It has been found to be particularly effective to protect a house against uninvited guests, spirit or otherwise, where these have become nuisance. To prevent such intrusion, the star should be drawn in the air and visualized at all the doors and windows of the house, taking care to have the point towards the outside, to create a barrier to entry.

To draw this star, start with the *right* hand at the *left* side of the body and make a large inverted V, ending it over on the *right* side of the body. From there, continue the figure by dissecting the first line of the inverted V. and then draw a line straight across or horizontally to dissect the second line of the original point, and continue back down to the left side from where it was started, as shown in the accompanying diagram.

As an added protection, a candle can be burned continuously

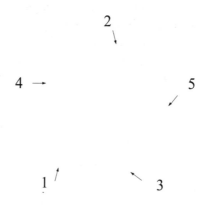

for several days, and a small container of salt placed in all four corners of each room while a window is left open a crack. Incense burned in the house also helps to cleanse it. These methods, we have found, effectively rid a house of unwanted ghosts or psychic projections.

### Beehive for Energy

Many people complain of a lack of energy and often ask if we have been given ways to help this condition. The tree meditation, which is described separately, is especially helpful and many people find that it is even more potent if they sit or stand against a living tree while doing it. We have also been given another symbol to use: one of those old-style rounded beehives which look like Eskimo igloos. The person needing energy imagines he is sitting inside the hive, rather side of the body. From there, continue the figure by dissecting the first line of the inverted V. and then draw a line straight across or horizontally to dissect the second line of the original point, and continue back down to the left side from where it was started, as shown in the accompanying diagram.

As an added protection, a candle can be burned continuously for several days, and a small container of salt placed in all four corners of each room while a window is left open a crack. Incense burned in the house also helps to cleanse it. These methods, we have found, effectively rid a house of unwanted ghosts or psychic projections.

### Beehive for Energy

Many people complain of a lack of energy and often ask if we have been given ways to help this condition. The tree meditation, which is described separately, is especially helpful and many people find that it is even more potent if they sit or stand against a living tree while doing it. We have also been given another symbol to use: one of those old-style rounded beehives which look like Eskimo igloos. The person needing energy imagines he is sitting inside the hive, rather like a Queen Bee, being fed and tended by the worker bees, breathing in deeply with each breath the energy he needs.

The pyramid acts in a similar way, but here it is the sunlight striking the top of it and raying down to the person within, which gives the extra energy.

### The Wave for Relaxation

Before giving this symbol, it is wise to inquire if the person has any fear of the sea or does not feel relaxed when near the ocean. If there is no problem, he is directed to lie down on an imaginary beach, right at the water's edge, with his feet pointing out to sea.

He is then told to imagine a long slow wave approaching him, gently washing over his whole body, stopping at his neck. As it recedes, he should consciously let go of all tension, and allow the wave to wash it out of him and away into the vast ocean to be dissipated. Many tense or nervous people have found this exercise so relaxing that they reported that they fell asleep while doing it.

## Symbols to Eliminate Faults

When a person is working on his various weaknesses or negative habits, he will often ask how he can more quickly free himself of them. Several methods have been suggested, and more arise as an increasing number of people use this method and ask to be shown what to do.

### The Authority Figure

With many people who have a clear picture of their own High C or other authority figures, such as the Cosmic Parents, it is a simpler matter to hand the weakness over to the figure, completely surrendering it. This surrender usually brings about release.

### The Torch

Some people, however, either cannot visualize such a figure or are not open to doing so and, for them, there are other ways. One of these is the torch, which is usually seen as very large and often permanently erected in a special place, such as a shrine, where the person can go for this release. I suggest that he find a symbol tn represent for him the unwanted aspect of himself which he wishes to eradicate, such as an angry-looking mask, or a clenched fist for anger, and hold this up to the flaming torch to be destroyed.

### The Flame in a Platter

Another way is to visualize a huge flat metal platter, in the middle of which burns an eternal flame, into which the symbolic object representing the unwanted negative quality can be thrown.

### Other Methods

Some people imagine they are stuffing their symbols representing negative habits into a furnace or flinging them far out into the ocean, or over a cliff or dropping them from a plane. There is no end to the variety of methods which are forthcoming in this way, each one being effective for the person choosing it.

### Figure Eight

I have already described what we call the Figure Eight exercise used as a preparation for cutting the connecting ties between parents and children. However, it has even more widespread uses and has become one of our most useful symbols. It can be used to free a person from anything or anyone which dominates him. Thus, many things can be placed in the opposite circle: a difficult person, habits, appetites and addictions, a restricting self-image and many more.

Alcoholics can use a symbol for drink such as a bottle; drug users, one for drugs such as a needle or cigarette. For those who want to lose weight, those foods which are a strong temptation, such as rich desserts like ice cream, pastries, cakes, candy, or other fattening foods, can be placed in the other circle. The Figure Eight can also be used to free a person from the domination of fear, anxiety, doubt, anger, envy, jealousy and many other negative emotions, as well as from the many limiting self-images which prevent people from living up to their potential, particularly those imposed by parents during childhood, comparison or competition with siblings, and memory of past failure in some activity. The list is limitless, but all that is needed is to find a symbol which successfully and convincingly portrays whatever it is which has gained control or power over the person.

The important thing to remember is that this exercise, like all the others, only works if it is practised regularly and long enough to impress the message on the subconscious mind of the person seeking to be free. Sometimes when someone has been visualizing the Figure Eight for a while there will come a time when the two circles will separate. This is an indication that the message has been understood and accepted and it is time to complete the separation.

There are many different ways to achieve the separation, as each person asks to be shown what to do. Some merely push the other circle containing the unwanted dominating factor far away, into the ocean, over a cliff, into outer space. Others need to set fire to it together with the contents, bury it deep in the earth, destroy it with acid or laser beams. The methods are limitless.

It is only important that the method satisfy the person involved, as it is his subconscious which must be impressed with the need to release him from the particular domination from which he suffers.

In this same way, many hangups' can be released very simply and effectively.

Let us look at negative self-evaluations such as 'I am weak, clumsy, stupid, unreliable', which lock a person into a pattern of behaviour and can severely limit him in all his daily activities. As soon as he is aware of such hindrances to being himself, he can usually very easily find a suitable symbol to fit his assumed negative role and start the Figure Eight exercise to begin freeing himself from it. Each time he uses the Figure Eight in this way, and achieves a measure of release, the more he will believe in its efficacy and, with each new success, it will accumulate more power and will work more effectively. So, once used, it will gather power and momentum and become a useful tool 'to free a person from any limiting attachments.

But, like all the other symbols, it must be practised daily on a regular basis, especially in the initial stages, by the person himself; it is not a magic wand which can be waved over a problem once or twice to make it disappear immediately and forever. However, it can be fun to do, as well as a challenge, if it is approached in the right way. It is the person's attitude which determines the outcome.

### Black and White Birds

One time when my daughter and I were working, after entering the reverie or waking-dream state, I became aware that I was walking a tightrope and had my arms out to my sides to balance myself. As I very carefully placed my feet alternately on the rope, a huge black bird attracted my attention over on my left side. I was afraid from the way it looked that it was about to attack me, so I lunged over to my left to push it away and, of course, lost my balance. As soon as I got back onto the tightrope again, I noticed a beautiful gleaming white bird on my right side, and was immediately so attracted to it that I impulsively leaned over to take hold of it, again losing my balance.

As usual, when in this state, I had been too involved in the inner scene to ask what it meant, but as soon as I did ask, I became aware that the black bird symbolized all those things I did not want to happen, or was afraid of, while the white bird represented all of the things I did want to happen and hoped for, i.e. my desires.

By reacting to either one, I lost my balance. I saw that the only way I could stay centred and therefore free was to resist the temptation to try to control either of the birds. So I started out again with my arms outstretched and with palms up and allowed either of the birds to alight on my hands, as and when they wished, accepting the black and white one equally.

I hasten to say that this visualization is far easier to write about than to put into practice; but once glimpsed, this picture makes it easier to remember not to react with strong negative emotions when life presents us with some experience we just do not want, or with too much excitement when our most cherished dreams come true. Either extreme destroys the inner calm we are trying to achieve and throws us off balance.

Baba told one of his favourite stories to illustrate this same point in a group interview in which we participated. He started by saying, "You all walk on such a bumpy road. How can you have peace?" Then he continued: "When you get what you want you are so happy, and go very high [illustrating with his hand raised above his head], but soon something will come along which does not please you and you go down very low [bringing his hand down to his feet]. See what a bumpy road you are walking on. Be happy whatever happens and you will walk on an even path and find peace.

*The Maypole*

I have often been asked if we have ever been given an exercise to use for a group meditation, or one which a family can use. The triangle which I have described earlier is excellent for family or group use. I was also shown that the usual method of having all the members of a group hold hands around a circle has the effect of bringing the group consciousness down to the lowest common denominator of the members of the specific group or gathering. A far more effective way of meditating in a group is for each person to imagine everyone reaching up to hold hands at a central point above the circle, representing the High C point where we are all one. It will easily be seen that in this way, each person will make a triangle with everyone else in the group, which raises the group consciousness to the highest common denominator, as it places the meditation under the direction of the united High-Selves. This enables each individual to receive whatever he needs at that particular time, whether it be healing, insight, awareness of hidden aspects of himself, solutions to problems, and much more.

There have been many variations on the original theme, and as many different symbols for using it, the maypole being the most effective and often the favourite. Most people have read about a maypole, seen one, or even participated as children in the traditional May Day festivities, in which the May Queen and the maypole dances play a big part.

For use as a symbol for group meditation each person should imagine or visualize a maypole firmly rooted in the ground, with different coloured ribbons attached to the top of the pole and hanging down around it. Each person then imagines walking up to the pole, choosing a ribbon, holding it in his hand, and returning to sit on the outer circumference of the circle. It is more interesting to ask each person which colour was picked, as it often gives insight into which is his strong or weak function.

As was explained in the chapter on the *mandala,* the maypole can also be used to equalize the four functions, in which case each person is encouraged to pick first the colour representing the weakest one and ask, as he sits holding it, that from the top of the pole will flow down into him via the ribbon whatever he needs to develop this function, noting any thoughts or pictures which may rome to mind to help. He should sit with palms up to receive this, nd allow glimpses to come to him of ways in which he can start eveloping the function rather than leaning on someone else who that function well developed.

By working with the maypole in this way people have reported that they receive healing, become more relaxed, feel stronger or more cheerful; in other words, they receive whatever it is they most need at that time. This visualization encourages people to rely on contact with their own High C instead of on other human beings.

We have observed that a tremendous energy is generated in

such a group meditation. It is as if each person has a lamp, with the energy from the High C as 'electricity' flowing down each of the many ribbons or wires and lighting up all the lamps in the room, so that the room is flooded with light and energy and all darkness is dispelled. This increased energy makes it possible for those present to receive even greater insights, clearer awareness, healing, a far greater state of relaxation and to enter a much deeper meditation than if they were meditating alone.

If the group is also interested in healing for others, each one may mention the name of someone requesting help, together with a very brief account of the problem, whether it be physical, mental, financial, or emotional. The whole group then imagines each of the people needing help sitting in the middle of the circle, as if leaning against the centre pole. Next, everyone in the group asks that healing, or any other needed help flow down from the universal High C and into the sick or disturbed person. This procedure is repeated all around the circle until all the requests for help have been dealt with.

As happens in the general meditation, people will sometimes receive quite explicit pictures, symbols, or other insights into the person being worked for, which often prove to be very helpful in understanding the condition, and in pointing the way to secure the necessary help. We have seen many quite startling results from such healing sessions.

As long as each member of the group consciously links up to the joint High C, none of the physical or psychological symptoms of the one seeking help can be taken on by anyone else, which often happens in healing groups where this precaution is not taken.

If there happens to be a member of the group who needs special help or healing himself, he should physically sit with palms up in title the centre of the circle while the others ask for healing or help for him, and open himself up as much as possible to the healing force, thus allowing it to take effect more directly and quickly.

## Further use of the triangle

The triangle has previously been described and its role explained as a basis for making contact with the High C at the beginning of every session, whether conducted on the conscious level or in the waking dream state. Like the Figure Eight, it also has other uses and, it too, is a very potent symbol.

Whenever anyone asks for help, the first thing I do is visualize a triangle connecting us both to the High C, and immediately ask up my side of it for the other person's High Self to heal, guide, or help in whatever way is needed and timely, and I suggest that the person do the same. We have been told that this is the utmost that anyone can do for another person.

Many people call to ask me to "Do triangles for me", for one thing or another, which is tantamount to asking me to hold a good thought or prayer for them. We are taught that it is acceptable to visualize the 'complete triangle for all those who are acquainted with it, or who sincerely seek contact with the High C, but we should not impose our will on those who are not open to this source. For them we visualize their side of the triangle as a dotted line, which they can make solid whenever they are ready to seek its aid.

Sometimes, 'running the triangle', as we often express it, is all that is needed to help a person if they are taking an examination, suffering from an illness, undergoing an operation, in the middle of an emotional crisis, involved in a divorce, or in any of the myriad of situations which force a person to reach out for help. However, it cannot be used as a magic wand and the person requesting help in this way must do his part, by visualizing it also, or he will become dependent on others to do it for him.

Quite often we are shown to erect the triangle above the Figure Eight with the points A and B at the centre of each circle. This makes an extremely effective symbol, as it prevents either person from dominating or projecting on to the other, while they both seek guidance from their joint High C.

### The Effect of Strong Emotions on the Atmosphere

The effect of strong emotions on the atmosphere and, thus, on people around us, was unexpectedly and beautifully illustrated one day when I was working with a woman who was suffering from great anguish over the recent death of her husband. She was much too distressed to work herself, so I tuned into our joint High C with a plea that something be given me with which to help to assuage her grief. I was immediately aware of a man whom I presumed was her husband. He was exhibiting signs of great excitement at the opportunity of communicating to her an exciting discovery he had made in the new dimension of being in which he now found himself. He informed us that he had discovered that he could project atmospheres, which he proceeded to demonstrate for me to describe to his wife. He asked me to watch the space between him and me on the inner scene and, as I did so, I became aware of an immense canvas or mural on which was being projected a flow of extraordinary combinations of colours and shapes. These were not flat or static like a painting or photograph, but constantly flowing, and three dimensional, the colours changing constantly as I watched.

He explained that he was projecting emotions, and with them he could 'paint with colour from every painter's palette these three-dimensional atmospheres'. He then erased the canvas and told me to watch as he was going to project anger.

I began to see a swirling circular space in the air, which spiralled and churned in shades of very dark red, brown and black, sucking into its centre everything around it, like a huge vortex. He quickly erased this and asked me which emotion I would like him to project next: I requested love. He began pouring an extraordinary shade of pink into the space I was watching, which expanded and opened up like a giant flower with the centre a deeper pink, from which were thrown out long floating tendrils like those of a sea anemone, each one caressing whatever it touched. He indicated that if we would both hold still he would project the tendrils towards us to envelop us with love.

Next came joy, an explosion of shades of yellow, orange and apricot, which did not stay together, but moved out in all directions. He pointed out that joy does not stay only with the one who is joyful, but reaches out to touch everyone around him. Then he wanted us to see anguish, which looked like an octopus spewing out shades of dark blue, indigo and dark red in long tentacles, which also extended out to touch everything within reach.

He went on to say that he is now aware that he and everyone

else is a creator, that anger makes it hard to breathe,while joy caresses, and that we should all be very careful of which emotions we project, as we have the choice of painting uplifting or depressing pictures. He created one last atmosphere which he called growth, and as I watched the space, very slowly there appeared a moving group of shades of pale yellow and green, starting at the bottom and gradually branching out like a tree of colour with the palest tips of yellow at the top of each branch. He left this picture of growth with his wife, saying, "Take growth as your theme; expansion and growth, and project joy instead of anguish."

## SYMBOLS TO USE FOR NEGATIVE EMOTIONS
### Fear

Fear seems to be one of the most crippling emotions and people will go to great lengths to try to be rid of it, yet they often report that it is extremely difficult to eradicate, perhaps because it is so pervasive. There are as many causes of fear as there are people in its grip and we have been shown several different methods to track down the origin.

Most frequently fear stems from childhood traumas, in which case we ask that the person seeking release be taken back in memory to the root cause or causes. As I have mentioned before, an authority figure such as Christ, Baba, or a personification of the High C may be called upon to accompany the person back into the traumatic incident to reassure and heal the child who still lives on within and who was once involved in the fear-producing experience. Sometimes, as in the case of my own fear of heights, the original cause lies back in a past life experience rather than in the present life, and was brought over as an unconscious memory.

Very often people report that they suffer from intangible fears which are even more frightening just because they are intangible, and fear of the unknown is one of the most prevalent forms of fear. For this type of fear we often use the corridor of doors and lead the fearful person to the door marked fear' and thus help him to discover the cause, as described in the chapter outlining this method.

Another useful method is to instruct the person to use the Figure Eight by placing either a specific fear or a symbol for fear, instead of a person, in the opposite circle to the one he occupies. This is often sufficient to stop intrusion by fear, especially if it is being picked up like an infection from someone else.

A helpful method to dispel fear of a special future event or activity, is the dress rehearsal. If the person with whom we are working is experiencing fear at the prospect of having to do something, or face someone, we first relax him, and then take him a step at a time through a rehearsal of the future event he is so dreading to face. We suggest that he ask to be shown all the various traps or problems which might possibly be involved and take him by surprise, and that he be shown how to deal with them ahead of time. Sometimes most surprising insights come out of such a session and many people report that they find they are so much more relaxed and self-assured when the time arrives for the actual confrontation that they invariably sail through it unafraid. This method is helpful when someone wishes to ask his boss for a raise, needs to fire an employee, or confront someone about a fault. It can also be used as preparation for giving a lecture or speech, taking an oral examination, or appearing at a trial. It is a most useful preparation for taking part in a play or presenting a proposal.

Sai Baba had a wonderful little story to illustrate his solution for dealing with fear of a wild animal or dangerous person. He advocates calling on, or recognizing the God Force within the person, animal, reptile, or other attacking creature, as it will respond very differently when that part is being called on and activated. Here is his story in full:

There was once a *guru* who told his disciple that God was in everything. The disciple believed the statement. That very day there was a royal parade. The king was the centre of attraction riding. on an enormous elephant. Ignoring the rules of safety for such parades, the disciple planted himself firmly in the path of the royal elephant, and paid no attention to the cries of warning that he would be trampled to death. Upon reaching him, the elephant lifted him and put him safely to one side. The disciple went to his *guru* and complained that although God was in both the elephant and himself, he had been unable to remove the elephant from his path and that, on the contrary, the elephant had removed him. The **guru** explained that it was merely a matter of the elephant having greater physical strength. He told the disciple that, had he not been looking at God in the elephant, the beast would have killed him just as a matter of ordinary work. However, since the disciple was looking at God in the elephant, God had lifted him safely out of harm's way. No animal, not even a cobra, will harm the person who sees God as the essential reality of the animal or the snake. The same is usually true as regards dangerous men, but there are some exceptions here because of *karmic* implications.'

I can vouch for the efficacy of calling on Baba as a symbol of the High C to dispel fear. When my husband and I were hijacked one year on a flight from India to England, I called on Baba and could not have been more amazed to discover that there was not a particle of fear anywhere in me, even though my conscious mind was reasoning that I should be filled with fear at being confronted by two villainous-looking Palestinians who were keeping us all covered with machine guns while they wired the plane preparatory to blowing it up.

Even after having been taken through one or more of the above exercises, some people still feel oppressed by fear and often say that it seems to lie deep within them, and that they have a fear of fear itself. For this situation, we have been given an exercise which we call the Jack.

### The Jack for Fear

One day we had been asked to work for a woman who was so full of fear that she could barely function in her daily life. As I relaxed into the reverie state I could see this woman very clearly, even though she was unknown to either of us who were working together that day. I could also distinctly see the fear inside of her like grey cobwebs or wisps of smoke. I started to reach out to try to take hold of some of it but discovered that it was slippery and, as soon as I thought I had hold of a strand of it, away it would float into another part of her. As I persevered, it floated further, so I asked help from the High C for a solution and received the direction to reach up above my own head and pull down what I would find there.

I did this mentally and discovered that I had taken hold of an object which looked like a jack from the children's game of that name except that this one was formed out of light, with the many rays emanating from a central ball of light. I was directed to pull it down so that it was level with my solar plexus and about six inches from my body. Then I was shown that the very centre of it was like a black hole, which had the ability to magnetically attract fear and pull it into its depths where the fear would be annihilated immediately. All I had to do was to allow the fears to come to my mind, verbalize them, and then literally let go of them, allowing the jack to draw them out and in to its centre.

We were told that this exercise was being given for use by anyone desiring to be rid of fear. So it was described to the woman who had asked for help, as follows:

1.  Imagine that you are reaching up above your head and touching a large jack (three-dimensional cross) like those used in the children's game. This one is composed of gold light, and the points are like rays of light.

2.  Pull it down as if it were on a pulley like some lamps suspended from the ceiling.

3.  Bring it down to about six inches away from your body in line with the solar plexus or diaphragm.

4.  As you breathe out, consciously let go of any fear of which you are aware, or just fear in general. It will be magnetically drawn into the middle of the jack which will, like a 'black hole', negate it.

5.  As you breathe in, consciously breathe in more light emanating from the points of the jack to replace the fear which you have dispelled and to heal the old trauma which caused it.

6.  When you finish each exercise period, push the imaginary jack up above your head on the pulley, ready for the next time you

may need it. While you are using it you can let go of any specific fears as they come to mind.

It may seem like a child's game, but it is intended to impress the subconscious part of your mind which is childlike, and not the rational conscious part.

She reported back the next day that she had had a very strong reaction the first time she used it. Her whole body shook violently as she began to release her fears, but she was not afraid as the accompanying feeling of relaxation was more complete than she could recall ever having experienced before, and she slept soundly that night for the first time in years. She has continued to use it whenever she feels the fear returning and finds that in this way she can easily trace it and let go of it quickly before it has had time to take hold of her again.

We have given this exercise to many others who have had this problem. All of those who have really used it conscientiously have reported very positive results.

## Guilt

Guilt is another paralyzing emotion which is very common and hard to release because the person who carries it is often unconscious of the cause. Like fear, the roots are often deep-seated and reach back into childhood, frequently resulting from overly strict parents who dealt out punishment which was too severe to fit the crime. Sometimes the section in the puberty rites meditation involving forgiving and asking forgiveness from the parents is sufficient to dispel the burden of guilt if it is related to the parents in any way.

There is also the possibility that guilt stems from a past life and has been brought over into the present one, in which case it can be traced back and faced, and absolution requested and received from the authority figure, or High C. Such a discovery can be most helpful in uncovering some of the old *karmic* debts which the person has incurred and he can then ask to be shown how best to work them out in his life.

If the guilt is caused by a conscious act, it is often that guilt which eventually drives the person to make the first step towards making amends. Then he may go a step further and, by an act of the will, determine to avoid repeating that particular mistake, asking for help from the High C to do so. In such cases, the guilt has served a purpose, for without it, the person would not be sufficiently aware of his negative behaviour to start to remedy it.

Some people feel guilty, not because of any act of their own, but because other people have made them feel guilty for some reason. Some of them say that they feel guilty just being alive, and we have found that this often ties in with the parents and can even go back to birth, especially if the mother died in childbirth or was rendered an invalid as a result of giving birth to the child. Many parents fail to realize that even a tiny baby can pick up negative emotions; particularly rejection and blame. Both of these directly attack the sense of security which is so desperately needed when the child first enters this strange world after being in the security of the womb for nine months.

Another cause of guilt is the disappointment of the parents over the sex of the child, a very common reaction and one that is often continued well into the child's life. The result is that the child feels that he is a mistake or a disappointment to his parents. In such a case, the guilt can often be relieved by having the person invoke the High C or other authority figure, and together go back in memory to the guilt-laden incidents and ask to be forgiven or granted absolution for himself or the parents. An imaginary ritual bath following this visualization will enhance the feeling of being cleansed.

However, even after the cause of guilt has been found and the forgiveness accepted, it is sometimes still hard for people to let go of an overlay of guilt, especially if it has been carried for a very long time and has become a habit. In such cases, we introduce an exercise we call the 'wet-suit'.

### The Wet-suit for Removing Guilt

This exercise came forth during work for someone who had been haunted by a vague, but no less heavy, feeling of guilt which he had been unable to shed despite the many methods he had tried in order to release himself from it.

As I looked at him on the inner level, he appeared to be clad in a shiny black wet-suit which reminded me of those worn by surfers. It fitted him like a second skin, constricting his movements and preventing him from breathing freely.

As soon as he was relaxed, I asked him to look down at himself to see if he could see this black covering over his entire body. He became very excited and said that he certainly could not only see it but feel it, and that it exactly matched the way he felt all the time — restricted and closed in.

I asked if he would like to be shown how to remove it and he fairly leapt at the chance. So I led him a step at a time to free himself from this unwanted covering, helping him with those parts which were difficult for him to reach. In his case, he could not remove the wet-suit all in one piece, but had to cut off a small piece at a time, naming the cause of each part as he proceeded. When he had finally succeeded in removing all of it, he had a pile of black scraps at his feet.

I asked him how he should destroy the scraps so that he would never be tempted to put those particular pieces back in place again. His reply was immediate: he would pour acid over the pile and, as he went ahead, I warned him to be sure that every shred was eaten up by the acid and that none were overlooked in his excitement over the opportunity to dispose of them. He worked hard and finally announced that every shred had disappeared without leaving even a stain.

I then suggested that he might like to take a shower or swim to wash off his entire body which had been covered by the wet-suit for so long. He chose to swim in the ocean so that the salt water could not only cleanse his body but stimulate and refresh it. I encouraged him to swim, splash and jump around to express his new-found freedom. He was really able to let go and romp in the water, so I suggested that he could also run up and down on the beach to expose his body to the sun and air and to further impress upon himself that he was now free.

At last he reported that he was tired and had collapsed. While he rested, I recommended that he check himself daily for a week, and thereafter once a week, to be sure that he had not taken back any parts of his old habit. I explained that should he see any evidence of the wet-suit, he could remove it immediately, pour acid over it, wash himself off in the ocean and air out his body as he had just done in the reverie and that it would take only a few minutes to do this once it had been removed the first time.

He later reported that he found he was able to recognize when he had accumulated a new layer of guilt and was able to rid himself of it at once after checking to see what had caused him to assume it again.

## Anger

Anger is one of the most destructive emotions, not only to the person being shaken like a rag doll in its grip, but to those who happen to be the unfortunate butt of its assault, and even to those who are unwilling spectators.

We asked for a symbol to help people to relinquish their anger and we were shown an image of a person who had swallowed a dragon which, imprisoned within, periodically writhes and spews out fire from frustration.

Anger stems directly from some block to the personal will or personal desire, so it is necessary first to investigate the type of incident which typically triggers anger in a person so that he has a better understanding of why anger has occurred. If it has been picked up as a habit from a parent, it can be relinquished at the time of cutting the ties to the parents. If it is the weapon wielded by a person with a strong will, then that behaviour must be looked at realistically so that the will of the ego may be given over and that of the High C sought instead.

Anger which is repressed is even more destructive. It is invariably unconscious and can erupt suddenly without warning. This condition is often the result of very strict parental control, where a child was never allowed to express anger and had literally to swallow it. In such cases anger can cause many kinds of physical ailments.

Yet another cause stems from the opposite situation, where the parents were too lenient and mistakenly showed their love for the child by allowing him to express anger whenever his wishes were not fulfilled, believing it to be harmful to deny him lest he interpret it as lack of love. That angry child is often very much alive in angry people and must be given the appropriate discipline by the person himself to replace that which the parents incorrectly administered or omitted.

When everything possible has been done to eradicate anger, such as voluntarily detaching from the personal unfulfilled desires, we give two different exercises which may help the person to release the core of the anger. In the first, the anger is described as a fiery dragon, which must be visualized as living within the person and ready to erupt whenever his personal will or desire are thwarted in any way. To get rid of this fiery beast, we guide the person to vomit it out and immediately kill it as soon as it is out in the light with a spear or sword plunged into its heart, in much the same way we deal with the dragon symbolizing the negative mother archetype. Killing the fiery dragon of anger is easier, because it is a personal and thus smaller monster. As soon as the monster has been killed and the carcass disposed of in whatever way is indicated, a small, smiling beatific cherub or some other personal symbol selected by the person must replace it. The cherub or other symbol represents a new start.

We have found that there are always a few people for whom this technique does not work. We asked to be given another symbol for them and were shown that some of these had brought anger over with them from a past life, but in a strange way. The creatures representing anger in this group were not dragons but mostly of the cat family: wild cats such as lions, tigers, or leopards. These did not symbolize anger springing from blocked desire like the dragon, but were linked to survival and connected to panic, rape, loss of life, danger and other crises. This anger occurs on a purely instinctive level and the victims are not conscious of why they have it; they are simply helpless in the grip of it. In some cases, they were attacked by a wild animal in a past life and were so frightened that their fear opened them up to identification with the animal that was attacking them. In some of these cases the people had been Christians sacrificed to the wild animals in Roman arenas as entertainment for the people. We were shown that these animals were not only starved for a time preceding each performance, but were teased and injured in order to make them mad with anger. The energy thus provoked was violent, aggressive and overpowering and it also induced in the participants strong sexual excitement as they identified with the strong masculine energy overcoming the weaker victims. Those in the crowd watching the display also derived a sadistic pleasure from seeing the helpless victims torn apart. Thousands of onlookers opened themselves up to this animal anger and, by reacting to it, have brought it over with them into later lives as have those whose job it was to torment the animals to arouse their anger.

Thus these fearful people have within them, instead of the symbols of the domestic instincts represented by the dog and cat, the wild attacking animals with which they had at one time been identified.

We were shown that other victims opened up in a different way. These were so frightened and in such physical and mental agony, that they tried to escape from their bodies and the pain being inflicted on them, craving a quick death which was preferable to present torment. They withdrew from the body as much as possible in an attempt to hasten death and escape from fear and pain and created a vacuum into which the fierce animal anger poured, bringing about a strange type of animal possession. Had they called on the God Force in the attacking animals, they might have been left unharmed like the Biblical characters Daniel and Abednego. If they had called on Christ or Jehova, they would have been helped to separate just enough from the body so that they felt no pain or fear, and yet were attached enough until death occurred naturally. To help these people, we were told to lure the animal of anger out of them by calling on the God Force in the animal. This calmed it and brought it slinking out, obedient to its own higher will.

We have also come across people who were attacked by an animal, usually a dog, during their present childhood. The shock and fear at such a sudden attack made them want to escape the body, which allowed the dog to invade them. In such cases, it is often preferable to take the person back to the actual scene, with his own High C or authority figure as support, comforter, healer of the old trauma, and to ask the person to speak to the God Force within the animal instructing it to emerge from the victim.

We were also shown that children who are taken to a circus or a zoo when they are still too young to understand can be overcome by the sight of some of the angry caged animals and invaded by them in a similar way.

Whenever we are shown a new method we always open it up for any others who have this same problem, and who are ready to be released, and we find that we will have several people with a similar problem in the same week.

## Jealousy and Envy

These two negative emotions are similar and are often confused in peoples' minds, but there are distinct differences between them. They both stem from greed and selfishness and are linked to desires and attachments.

Jealousy springs to life in a person when he is faced with the possibility that someone may take something or someone away from him which he values. He then tries hard to guard what he considers his property, hating the one who threatens to rob him. Envy is born of lust, and tempts a person to reach out to grasp something belonging to someone else which he covets. These two emotional reactions are closely linked, as one person jealously guards his possessions, while the other envies him for owning them.

The underlying greed common to both is one of the most constricting emotions. It impedes the natural flow on all levels: body, mind, emotions, and spirit, and also affects those around the greedy person. Greed signifies holding on, rather than letting go and flowing with the basic rhythm of life.

The first task in dealing with these negative emotions is to try to determine what triggers them in a person and whether they are the result of basic character weaknesses or of circumstances or childhood experiences. In some people they can stem from insecurity and a desperate need to hold on to people or objects for support and comfort, rather than seeking security from the High C.

If this is the case, the Figure Eight can be used around the person and a symbol representing whatever he is tempted to hold onto so tightly that he fears it will be taken from him. This exercise will lessen the hold and he can then be taken into a session to release himself from his crutch and make contact with the High C.

Symbols representing envy, greed and jealousy can also be handed over to the personification of the High C, or destroyed by burning them in the torch, or the eternal flame.

### The Worm in the Apple

Because the emotions of envy and jealousy create such serious problems for so many people, my daughter and I asked during a work session if we could be shown a symbol to help people to eradicate them.

I was startled to be shown a beautiful, shiny red apple which looked perfectly developed and ripe. I was directed to look inside it and not be fooled by its outer appearance. When I did this, I was shocked to see that a worm had burrowed deep into it and had eaten its way to the very core, reducing the apple to a hollow shell. We then understood that jealousy and envy, like the worm, both borrow deep into a person's heart until it, too, becomes empty and hollow, just as I had seen the apple.

I next saw a big, fat, puffy red heart, like those on some Valentine cards, and was shown that anyone desiring to rid himself of these negative emotions should visualize this as a symbol of his own heart. He can then be helped to cut or dig down into it with whatever instrument he is shown to use, until the worm is exposed, and he can lift it out and exterminate it in any way he likes.

The worm must be replaced by something which the person chooses as a symbol of love and generosity. These symbols vary with each person and range all the way from maraschino cherries and strawberries to cupids, angels, lotuses, and lights. An important part of the process is for each person to discover the most meaningful symbol for him and not copy others. When found, the symbol can be used as a daily visualization to impress his subconscious mind with the new message of love, replacing the old envy and jealousy.

## Greed

Most of the negative emotions have as their basis greed, which is the essence of attachment to the desires of the ego, expressed as 'me' and 'mine'. Greed also usurps the place of the High C as it gives an illusion of security in tangible objects. Since these are not lasting, they never completely satisfy or fulfill, but breed insecurity, the very condition they are relied upon to eliminate.

Because greed is the foundation of most negative emotions and therefore affects both personal situations and world problems, we have found that it is one of the most difficult to exterminate. We have been given many techniques to loosen its hold, because since it is often deeply entrenched within the very structure of a person, it has to be attacked from all sides. Some of these techniques have been mentioned in the appropriate contexts. We needed a more comprehensive symbol like those for anger and fear so we asked for this during a session.

We were shown a grotesque picture of a head with a huge gaping mouth, and a ring of outstretched and grasping hands sticking out all around the neck like a collar or necklace. There appeared to be no body except for what looked like a tapeworm attached to the head and leading down into a storage place in the subconscious.

We were shown that, like the tapeworm, greed lives inside its host, devouring everything it can get hold of but leaving the host completely unsatisfied and always hungry for more. Thus it creates a vicious circle which must be broken if the host is to be free of such negative infestation. The head, tapeworm and storehouse, must be cut out and destroyed by fire or some other appropriate means, as indicated by the High C. The space it occupied inside the person must then be filled with light or some other replacement, as directed, to ensure that it will not recur. The storehouse needs to be looked at very carefully to determine the types of things which bring out the greed in each person so that he can consciously release their hold on him.

## Teaching Pictures

A large collection of 'teaching pictures' has accumulated over the years from the working sessions. I will include a sampling of these as they are so universal in their appeal and application. Often we will be shown a picture or scene, as if in a play, to illustrate a point or give insight into a situation or personal problem for ourselves or someone for whom we are working and later discover that it is equally applicable for others with similar problems. In this way, each person's problem can help other people, linking them all in an invisible partnership of giving and receiving.

Sometimes merely being shown one of these pictures gives sufficient insight and understanding for the person to be able to change his actions and affect his situation accordingly. Often when we are shown what to do to change ourselves or our attitudes, we have the choice of continuing in the same pattern or correcting it ourselves.

### Tape-measure and Snake

When I first started to work in this way, I became aware that my conscious mind would often get in the way so I asked what I could do to prevent this. I immediately saw, on my right side, a spring tape-measure symbolizing my mind, always busy measuring everything I saw. I was directed to pull it out as far as possible and then release it so that it sprang back into its case with a sharp click. This became a preliminary exercise for me before trying to make contact with my subconscious mind and it worked so well that we have often given it to others who have experienced the same difficulty.

A little later I realized that not only was my mind a problem while I worked in this way, but that my emotions would often intrude and block the flow of images or teachings. So, again, I asked to be shown what to do to put them temporarily at rest. This time I saw a tree with a snake hanging over one branch with its head towards the earth. The snake was a symbol for my emotions and I was directed to wind it very gently until it was coiled into a spiral along the branch of the tree with its tail in its mouth, completely contained. I realized as I used it that this picture was perfect; as the tree symbolized the impersonal self with the snake safely coiled up in its branches so there could be no further intrusion by my emotions to block the flow of images which could then be evaluated impersonally.

### The Knotty Pine Fence

During one session, the inner picture was of a high knotty pine fence, on each side of which was a wise looking owl. One of the owls reminded me of a Methodist minister with whom I was working while the other one looked like a psychologist who was also working with me. Neither could see the other over the high fence separating them, but I saw that if one of the knots in the fence at their head level was pushed out they would be able to see one another through this small space. I was then shown that the hole symbolized this work through which the minister could look at the psychological aspects and the psychologist the spiritual ones instead of concentrating only on their own viewpoint.

### The Swinging Door

Another picture along the same lines was of a swinging door between the Eastern and Western philosophies. The swinging door symbolized this way of working which is a synthesis of the two philosophies. In this work, those who are primarily Western in their attitudes and beliefs are exposed to Eastern methods, and vice versa, so that eventually the two may meet and see that they have many common bonds.

### The Two Clocks

My friend and I were working with another married couple, she with the wife and I with the husband. The couple's problem was that sometimes they were in perfect rhythm with each other and at other times they seemed to be out of step. They were anxious to find a way to be more harmonious all the time. This appears to be a universal wish, so we asked to be shown anything which could help.

We saw two clocks of the type having a pendulum swinging back ~ and forth inside a glass case. When we first saw this picture, the pendulums were moving back and forth at the same rate but, very gradually, we observed a barely perceptible change as one of the pendulums seemed to be moving ahead of the other. After a while, as we watched, this became more obvious until their rhythms were far apart. However, this did not last and we saw that they started to move back towards a closer rhythm until they again appeared to be in perfect synchrony.

We were then shown that no two people are exactly alike and that it is impossible and unrealistic to expect that they can always be in perfect agreement. Neither is it advisable for one of the partners to force the other to assume his rhythm or to try to achieve the same as his partner, in either case, forcing one or the other to be untrue to himself. When both of them align their wills to that of the High C, each can find his own rhythm and accept the distance between them when it occurs, thus protecting each one's individuality.

*The Two Snakes*

A woman who had been married a long time to a man who was quite a challenge to her was shown a picture of two snakes writhing together on the ground. At first she thought they were engaged in a mating embrace but, to her surprise, she saw that, as they interacted, each one was gradually losing its skin. Later she read that it is indeed a fact that snakes help one another to remove their old tight skins in this way when they have outgrown them. She realized that some of the struggles between her and her husband would actually achieve this same purpose if they could but relax and allow it to happen.

*The Tulip and the Chrysanthemum*

At another time, when we were working for another couple, we were shown that each could be likened to a plant. One was like a tulip and the other a chrysanthemum. We could easily see that deep within each of us is our true pattern or seed of the person into whom we should develop. However, these inner potentials often fail to develop freely and normally. There are many different factors involved: each plant needs to be planted in the right type of soil, in shade or full sunlight, or filtered light, and each has individual water and food and fertilizer requirements. People, like plants, thrive when all of these requirements are met but, in most cases, certain adjustments have to be made. In the case of the couple for whom we were working, the two partners obviously had very different needs and would be faced with the necessity of a great deal of adjustment if their marriage was to be a fulfilling relationship.

## Dog and Cat

At one time, near the beginning of our partnership, my friend and I were working with a married couple, she with the wife and I with the husband. The man was so withdrawn that I was at a loss to know how to help him to open up even enough to tell me his problems. So, the next time my friend and I worked together, I asked to be shown anything which would help me to work with him.

Immediately a vivid picture of a wide and rapidly flowing stream flashed onto my inner screen. I saw that a tree trunk had fallen across it, forming a bridge, in the middle of which crouched a cat which was obviously terrified as it watched the fast-moving water so close beneath it. It was far too frightened to continue on across to the safety of the opposite bank, but equally afraid to retrace its steps and return to the side from which it had come. So there it was, as if glued to the tree trunk, paralyzed and unable to make a move in either direction. Then I caught sight of a boisterous cocker spaniel as it leapt into the stream and started to swim over towards the tree, splashing water all over the poor cat as it approached. This caused the cat to freeze even more as it clung desperately to its precarious perch.

I realized that this was a perfect picture of this couple and their individual attitudes to life. The wife was an outgoing, enthusiastic and demonstrative puppy dog-type of woman who romped through life, while her husband was a typical introverted cat-like man too scared to enter the stream of life. Then we realized that this metaphor could be applied to many people and, from then on, we always tried to determine which people were more like dogs and which ones were more cat-like. We found that this made it a great deal easier to understand how to handle each one.

Shortly after this, one of my own cats illustrated this point even further. She strayed out of the house and up into the hills, presumably so frightened at the unfamiliar outside world that she was scared to return home, even to eat, and would not let any of us approach her. It took several days of the utmost patience to entice her back with a bowl of food which, at first, I placed quite far from the house, but, each day, gradually brought it in closer until she was coming to eat at the back door. Finally I was able to reach down and pick her up. At first she fought from fright but a few strokes behind her ears relaxed her so that she could accept being home again.

When working with extremely introverted people, it is often necessary to proceed cautiously, offering small quantities of help and encouragement until their confidence has been won and their fears decreased.

The division of people into dogs and cats is also very helpful in daily life when meeting various types of people, as it presents a quick way of deciding how to relate to them. Cat-like people respond best when approached gently and slowly, and really prefer to be allowed to make the first overture themselves. They cannot be overwhelmed with attention and affection or taken unawares. On the other hand, dog-like people love to be hugged and often will make the first move as they also love to lavish affection on those they love as well as to receive it.

Naturally, a person is more balanced if he is able to alternate between these two extremes, depending on those with whom he is interacting. We have had several Siamese cats who are in many ways quite like dogs; so they have come to symbolize the middle way; neither too extroverted nor disproportionately introverted.

*The Three Mountains*

One time when we were working I had an inner experience which illustrated for me the balancing of the two functions of intellect and emotion. I was aware that in my inner scene I was jumping back and forth between two large mountains. As I landed on one, I saw that it was composed of hard sharp rocks and crags on which I could be cut and bruised if I stayed for too long a time; so I quickly jumped back onto the other one. I then discovered that this one was covered with deep snow into which I could sink and be smothered if I remained on it too long. So back I jumped again to the craggy one, and so on, back and forth between them. I began to get very tired and asked the meaning of this experience. I was shown that the craggy mountain symbolized the intellect and the snow-covered one the emotions, and that I had been alternating between these two ways of handling situations.

I was then directed to look between these two mountains and, as I did, I saw to my surprise that there was a third mountain which I had not even suspected was there. It was not as high as the other two and, when I asked what it symbolized I received the answer that it represented a state of knowing, neither solely feeling nor entirely thinking, but in which both operated together. I was also shown that the third mountain was composed of the dead bodies of all my released desires, desires that certain things occur as well as that other things not occur. As I looked at it more closely, it reminded me of a coral reef which is composed of the skeletons of the tiny sea creature known as a coral polyp. This mountain was beautifully green and dotted with hundreds of lovely little wild flowers and, as soon as I was willing to land on it instead of continuing to jump back and forth between the other two, I discovered that it continued to grow higher and higher as I let go of my desires. Eventually I saw it could reach the sun, which is a symbol in our work of the God Force, and that I could then merge in union with it and be released from the constant pull of the pairs of opposites which keep us chained to the earth scene.

### The Human Dog on a Leash

A friend of mine, who lives at a distance, calls from time to time to ask for help with whatever is troubling her. On one of these occasions, she told me that several weeks earlier her boss had promised her a different and much more interesting position in the large organization in which they both worked. He had made no further mention of it so she had called his office a few times to find out what was happening as she was becoming frustrated by the continued uncertainty. She told me that he had not returned her calls which frustrated her even more. She was now asking if we would check to see if there might be more she could do.

During a session in which we were working for others, I saw my friend on the inner screen and noticed that she seemed to be holding in one hand what looked like a long dog leash on which she was tugging impatiently. I followed it to see where it led and saw a man on the other end instead of a dog and every time she pulled on the leash, his attention was jerked away from whatever he was doing and I could see that he was becoming very nervous, and irritated. I was then shown that she must drop this imaginary leash and give it over to her own High C, releasing it entirely a asking to be shown what to do next. She did this faithfully each day and reported back a little later that the man had called her and, in the friendliest manner, had said he was sorry for the delay but was now ready to discuss a proposal with her.

We have been given many more symbols and pictures during the years of work with this method and still more are being discovered as new people participate in the work. I have described examples for specific needs and problems to point the way to further discoveries by those who will be attracted to this type of work. Once again, I must stress that it is important to remember that the symbols themselves are not magic wands but tools which must be used daily, in a disciplined fashion, to impress the subconscious mind with the need for new patterns of thought, feeling and behaviour.

*Yin Yang*

A very helpful symbol for balancing the male and female aspects in a person of either sex is the ancient Chinese symbol *Yin Yang*. In order to use it the person is instructed to imagine or visualize standing astride the symbol as if it were drawn on the ground, with the left foot over the white dot in the dark side, and the right foot on the dark spot on the light side, concentrating on seeking a balance between the two within himself.

YIN YANG SYMBOL

# CONCLUSION

In this book I have shared a sampling of the teaching, techniques and symbols which have been received over the years by using this method. As I started to write I quickly realized that there is far too much material to fit into one book. Therefore each subject or aspect has been only lightly touched on, and a minimum of case histories included.

It can easily be seen that this work is not a crystallized discipline, but is continuously evolving and expanding as it is used by more people who choose to turn within to seek answers to their questions from the High C. Even as I write, new insights, symbols and techniques are continuing to be uncovered.

I hope the basic steps as outlined in the book are sufficiently clear for those who are interested to follow, as only personal experience of the various techniques will give a real picture of how they work in daily life.

It was not until I started to write the book that I saw that there were well-defined steps and a very clear pattern which could be followed and adapted to each person's needs.

The sequence of steps may be varied from one person to another, and this will usually be indicated by his dreams. If his Inner Child shows up in a dream ahead of the Inner Enemy, then the sessions should be placed in that order. If the reverse, then it should be adjusted accordingly.

If a person had particularly negative parents, the tree exercise should be given to him to link him to his Cosmic Parents before he attempts to cut the parental ties.

The constant use of the triangle is essential so that the High C is consulted at every step along the way. If this one rule is adhered to, the correct sequence will be indicated.

I sincerely hope that all those who have read this far and are interested in experiencing this method will derive as much fulfillment from their participation as I and others who have used it have enjoyed both in the past and now.

I am happy to have shared this much and hope it can now be used to benefit many people than I could ever reach personally. I release it into the hands of the High C from whence it emanated and hope that all who are drawn to use it will find it to be a continuing adventure inwards.

# INDEX

abortion, 77
adoption, 13, 17
aggression, 72, 73 107, 162
alcohol, 7, 10, 93, 97, 147
amnesia, 93
anger, 10, 42, 53, 66, 77, 95,
    125—126, 140, 147, 153,
    161— 163
anima, 38, 69—75, 105, 114
animals, 5, 95, 155, 162—163
    caged, 5,9, 162—163
    wild, 155,162
animus, 38, 69—75, 78, 114
archetypes, 35, 48, 71—72, 94,
    96, 115, 161
atmosphere, 152—153

Baba (see Sathya Sai Baba)
balance, 41, 74, 102-109, 109, 114,
    142, 147—148, 171,
    163—175
black cloud, 87—90
black hole, 157
black widow spider, 35, 37, 72
bonding
    at birth, 12
    at marriage, 73—75
bonds
    between family members,
    75—76
    between past loves, 78—82
    Buddha, 54, 137

Christ, 51, 55, 61, 77, 101, 138,
    153, 162
cigarette/s, 97, 147
compassion, 8, 50, 80, 136
Corridor of Doors, 123-126, 153
Cosmic Father, 48—53, 94, 115

Cosmic Mother, 48—53, 94, 115
Cosmic Parents, 45—52, 94, 146,
175
criticism, 8, 14, 34, 40—42, 53,
    68, 106, 140, 142
crystals, 108-109, 117
cutting ties, 9—10
    for other people, 80—82
    from old loves, 78—80
from other family members,
    78—79
from predominating factors,
    147—148
to and for a dying person,
    127—138
to other relationships,76—84
    to parents, 11- 21, 22—34
cyclops, 38
Cylinder of Light, 86, 141

death, 10, 14, 17, 62—63, 70,
    77, 77– 82, 82– 83, 127– 138
    death rites, 12, 127—138
decision, 140-141
dragon, 33, 36—37, 157—159
dream/s, 20, 40, 53, 78, 92—94, 95,
96, 98—99, 101, 111—122,
125, 130
(see also waking dream) drugs, 7,
8,10, 90, 97, 108, 147

envy, 147, 162—164
Earth Mother, 50
exercises, see Visualization Exercises

family cloud/s, 84—86
father, 34, 37, 53, 60—67, 60—67, 68
negative, 35—38
(see also Cosmic Father and Solar
Father)

fear, 10, 38, 95, 96, 99, 123—124, 140,
    147, 154—158, 166—167,
    170-171
feeling, 99, 109, 171—172
Figure Eight, 4, 13—18, 59, 70,
    76, 87, 93, 113, 129, 137—138,
    139, 144—145, 152, 154, 164
    instructions for visualizing,
    15—19
flying, 107—108
forgive/ness, 29—30, 65—67, 77,
    78—79, 83, 137, 158—159
foster parents, 14
    free will, 6

Ganesh, 54
giant/s, 35, 38
God, 82, 131, 155—156
    aspects of, 54, 138
God Force, 54, 155, 162—163, 171
guilt, 58—62, 66, 82, 95, 99, 123,
    136—137, 140, 158—160

homosexuality 71-72, 117-119

incest, 57, 60, 78
inherited family cloud/s, 87—89, 90
inherited ink blot, 90—91
Inner Child, 56—68, 99
Inner Enemy, 92—97, 115
Inner House, 98-101
insanity, 93
insecurity, 6, 48, 108, 124, 164
intellect, 102—109, 125, 171
intuition, 102—110

jealousy, 11, 41, 42, 60, 123, 125,
    147, 164—165
Jesus, 9, 137
    (see also Christ)
Jung, Carl, 38, 69

karma, 108, 158
Krishna, 54
Kuan Yin, 54

laziness, 42
loneliness, 124, 132
lovers, 11, 69
lust, 163

Madonna, 137
    (see also Virgin Mary)
mandala, 102-107, 140, 142, 150
marriage, 57—59, 62—63, 72—74,
    80-82, 106, 167-169
    inner marriage, 114
mate, 72, 81-82
    choice of, 57, 69
maypole, 109, 140, 149-151
meditation, 100, 110, 135
    group meditation, 149—151
Medusa, 71—72
miscarriage, 77
Mohammed, 137
monster/s, 35, 38, 96—97, 161
mother, 66, 70, 77—78, 83—84, 96
    negative, 35—38
    (see also Cosmic Mother and
        Earth Mother)

octopus, 35, 37, 73, 84, 153
ogre/s, 35, 38
over-eat, 45—u, 77

parents
    cutting ties to, 23—34
    negative archetypes, 35—38
    positive & negative attrib-utes
        (of), 37—44
    ties to, 11—19
    (see also Cosmic Parents!
        Mother/Father)
past life, 88, 92, 125—126, 136,
    153, 161—163

pentacle, 87, 143—144
　(see also under symbols)
pride, 11
programming, 12,39,60, 118, 139
　destroying negative, 43—47
protective symbols, 140—145
　(see also under symbols)
puberty, 12, 73
　puberty rites, 12—13, 22—34,
　　48, 64—65, 158
pyramid, 87, 108—108, 141—142,
143

rape, 162
rebellion, 13, 40—47, 69, 72, 134
rebirth, 11
reincarnation, 71-72, 79
rejection, 14, 49, 52—53, 57, 64—67,
　74—75, 122, 155
relaxation, 22—28, 66
　suggestions for, 25-28
remarry, 63
resentment, 14, 53, 66, 77
reverie, xi, 38, 119, 126, 128, 136, 150,
158
(see also waking dream)
　rhythm, 77, 167—168
ritual/s, x, 13, 14, 35, 38,
　44—45, 52, 76, 77, 79, 87,
　91, 128—131, 159

Sai Baba
　(see Sathya Sai Baba)
SathyaSaiBaba, 54, 77,118, 142,
　149, 154, 155—156
security, 6, 11, 53, 73, 105, 107,
　141, 142, 164
sensation, 102-109
sex, 28, 57, 59—60, 68,
　71—72, 74, 162
　abuse, 57, 60
　compulsive, 59
　fear of, 57

the triangle in relation to, 74
unwanted sex of child, 61, 159
Shiva, 54
shyness, 41
siblings, 78—79, 147
Solar Father, 50
sphere, 87, 103
　(see also under symbols:
　　balloon & bubble)
subconscious, x, 16, 19—20, 25,
　33-34,47, 82,91,95,104,
　106,109, 112,115, 119, 140, 147-148,
　157, 165, 166, 172
suicide, 88-93
symbol/s, 140, 174
　Figure Eight, 14–19, 147–148
mandala, 102-110
maypole, 109, 149-151
pyramid, 108—109, 142—143
Protective Symbols,
　141—146
　balloon or bubble, 141
　beehive for energy, 145—146
　crossroads, 144
　cylinder of light, 142
　pentacle or five-pointed
　　star, 87, 144-145
plate glass screen, 142
　pyramid, 144 –145
　scales, 142–144
　umbrella or sun-shade, 142
wave for relaxation, 146
Symbols to Eliminate Faults, 146—
151
authority figure, 146
black and white birds, 148—149
Figure Eight, 147—148
flame in platter, 147
maypole, 149—151
torch, 146—147
triangle, 152
Symbols for Negative Emotions,

154–172
    jack for fear, 156—158
    symbol for greed,165—166
    tapesty level, 7—9
    wet suit for guilt, 159— 160
    worm in the apple,164—165
    (see also TeachingPictures)
*Teaching Pictures,* 166—173
    dog and cat, 169—170
    human dog on leash, 171—172
    knotty pine fence, 167
    swinging door, 167
    tape measure and snake,
       166-167
    three mountains, 170— 171
    tulip and chrysanthe-mum,
       168-169
    two clocks, 167—168
    two snakes, 168
    yin yang, 172-173

*Tibetan Book of the Dead,* 127, 137
ties, 9—11, 61—62,75—84,
    129—132
    to parents, 12—15
torch, 146—147
tree, 48—51, 141, 145
    tree exercise, 49—51

triangle, 2, 5, 27, 31,45, 54, 59,
    72, 74, 76, 134, 136, 139,141
    further uses of, 152
    in marriage, 106
    in sexual experience, 74
    running the triangle, 31,142

Virgin Mary, 54, 55, 61, 79—80
Vishnu, 54
    Visualization exercises
    connecting to Cosmic Parents,
       51—54
    Corridor of Doors, 124—125
    dispersing black clouds,
       89—90
    dispersing ink blots, 90—91
    Figure Eight, 14—19
    jack for fear, 158
    mandala, 105—107
    maypole, 150
    puberty rites, 28—35
    relaxation, 25—28
    tree, 49—51
    triangle, 76

waking dream/s, 12,44,54,90, 103,
    148—149
    (see also reverie)
witch/es, 35, 37

yin yang, 172-173

## ABOUT THE AUTHOR

Phyllis Krystal is a psychotherapist. She was born in England but lives and works in Germany where she has developed her own techniques of psychotherapy. For over Forty years, she has been developing a counseling method using symbols and visualization techniques that help people detach from external authority figures and patterns in order to rely on their own Higher Consciousness as guide and teacher. To teach the method, Krystal gives lectures and seminars in the U. S., Europe, England, New Zealand, Tasmania, South America and Australia. She is a devotee of Sathya Sai Baba, a world-renowned avatar living in India whose teachings and personal influence have been an inspiration. She is the author of *Cutting More Ties that Bind, Cutting the Ties that Bind - Workbook, Sai Baba: The Ultimate Experience, Taming Our Monkey Mind, Ceiling on Desires and Let's Thank God.*

# OTHER BOOKS BY PHYLLIS KRYSTAL

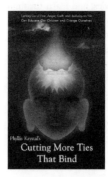

### Cutting More Ties That Bind

This is the sequel to "Cutting the Ties that Bind" and contains advanced information that can be used to release ourselves from more complex systems that program behaviour. These include familiar and national custom – things we do without even thinking about them. This is the book that will make us "see" what we are doing; it will help us release thought forms; it will help us be the kind of parents we wish we had! This is a book of effective self- awareness that opens the door to a lifestyle of self-assured and happy people.

201 Pages | ISBN 978-81-7899-093-8 | ₹ 160

### Cutting The Ties That Bind - Work Book

Well illustrated, concise, step by step explanation of the techniques described in *Cutting the Ties that Bind* and *Cutting More Ties that Bind*. Clearly shows the methods of self fortification against malicious influences, and liberating oneself from stifling thought and energy. Can be used for tie cutting with individuals and groups. An invaluable companion to Krystal's other books. The work book is self contained and can be used independently. Handy and effective.

89 Pages | ISBN 978-81-86822-35-6 | ₹ 170

### Cutting The Ties That Bind - Cards & Posters

Free your way to Happiness and Health

• Powerful visualization techniques in these 14 harmoniously colored cards & posters help you to Connect to Hi-C — Your True Self, the Source of Security, Power and Joy.

• Bring the shape of your complexes and their initial causes (for instance, imposed negative Parental Archetypes) from the unconscious mind into awareness. With guidance from your Higher Consciousness you demolish them yourself. Your personality blooms into full potential.

14 Cards | ISBN 978-81-86822-35-6
Cards ₹ 150 | Posters ₹ 600

**More books on next page ▶**

## Cutting the Ties of Karma

Open the pages of the *Cutting the Ties of Karma*, the latest edition of the 'Cutting the Ties' series, and learn through Phyllis Krystal's teachings and wisdom that your past doesn't have to bind you to your future. Learn to identify what your bad patches are through dream work, figure out your karma in relationship to significant people in your life, and ultimately, eliminate the bad karma from your life. *Cutting the Ties of Karma* makes possible a new patchwork of life from which to unfold.

197 Pages | ISBN 978-81-7899-007-5 | ₹ 160

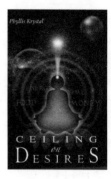

## Ceiling on Desires

This book is written to help explain the Ceiling on Desires program, and to show how eliminating waste and negative personal characteristics of the ego can impact our desires. The basic material has been taken from an interview with Baba in January, 1983, devoted entirely to this program, various subsequent group interviews with Baba, his public lectures, some personally heard, as well as others published in the *Sanathana Sarathi*, plus his daily talks to devotees during the celebrations of his 60th birthday and 4th World Conference in November, 1985.

164 Pages | ISBN 978-81-7899-090-3 | ₹ 150

## Let's Thank God

This "small book" contains selections of Sathya Sai Baba's sayings on the many subjects that His teachings cover. Many people enjoy these little gems, His sayings, and even quote them frequently, but find it very difficult to apply them in their daily life. The interpretations by well known Psychotherapist and long time Baba's devotee Phyllis Krystal show with examples how His teachings can be put into practice in daily life.

96 Pages | ISBN 978-81-7899-020-2 | ₹ 90